불교영어

초급

대한불교조계종 교육원 불학연구소 편찬

조계종
출판사

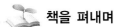 **책을 펴내며**

　오늘날은 바야흐로 세계화시대입니다. 이에 따라 국내외에서 영어로 불교를 포교할 일이 많이 생겼습니다. 그리고 템플스테이나 각종 행사와 모임 자리에서 외국의 불자들이나 일반인들에게 한국불교를 소개하거나, 불교를 소재로 한 대화를 나눌 일이 많아졌습니다.

　이러한 필요에 따라 본 연구소에서는 《불교영어 초급Ⅰ》을 펴내게 되었습니다.

　이 책의 내용과 주요 구성은 1부 〈영어회화〉, 2부 〈불교 교리〉, 3부 〈한국불교 역사와 문화〉의 세 부분으로 나뉘어 있습니다.

　특히 1부 〈영어회화〉 편은 사찰에서 일상적으로 가장 많이 접하는 주제와 상황을 6개의 장으로 나누고, 각 장마다 가능한 대화 상황을 6~7 단원으로 수록하였습니다. 대화의 주요 내용은 템플스테이, 사찰안내, 불교의식, 사찰생활, 수행, 한국불교 역사와 문화를 다루고 있습니다. 대화의 주체와 내용들이 스님들 중심으로 엮은 것은 이 책이 승가대학의 스님들 교재로도 활용되기 때문입니다.

　본 교육원에서 추진하고 있는 불교영어 교재는 총 6권으로서 《불교영어 초급Ⅰ》, 《불교영어 초급Ⅱ》, 《불교영어 중급Ⅰ》, 《불교영어 중급Ⅱ》, 《불교영어 고급Ⅰ》, 《불교영어 고급Ⅱ》입니다. 이 중 《불교영어 초급Ⅰ》, 《불교영어 초급Ⅱ》는 2012년에 발행할 예정이며, 나머지도 매년 발행될 수 있도록 준비해 나갈 것입니다. 《불교영어 초급Ⅰ》은 처음 나오는 불교영어 교재인 만큼 여러모로 미흡한 면이 있으리라 봅니다. 이러한 점들은 지속적으로 보완하도록 하겠습니다.

　끝으로 이 교재가 승가대학의 스님들뿐만 아니라 여러 불자들이 영어로 한국불교를 소개하고, 불교를 포교하는 데 많은 도움이 되기를 기대합니다.

2556(2012)년 2월
대한불교조계종 교육원 불학연구소

1부 〈영어회화〉 편은 스님들이 사
찰에서 일상적으로 가장 많이 접
하는 주제를 6개의 장으로 나누고
각 장마다 가능한 대화 상황을
6~7 단원으로 수록하였습니다.
6개의 주제는 템플스테이, 사찰안
내, 불교의식, 사찰생활, 수행, 한
국불교 역사와 문화입니다.

Words and Phrases
문법 정리와 어휘 활용법

본문과 관련된 내용의 문법을 한번
더 정리하면서 그와 관련된 다양한
표현의 회화를 익히도록 했습니다.
핵심 문법 패턴을 외워 여러 상황의
단어를 활용해보면 자연스러운 대
화가 완성될 것입니다.

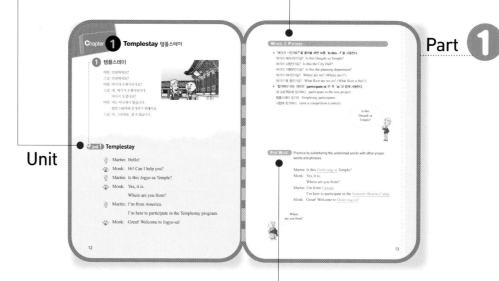

Unit

Part 1

Pair Work 말하기

한글 회화와 영어 회화, 그 단원에 쓰인 단어와 구문
의 해설, 그리고 파트너와 함께 관련 회화를 더 연습
할 수 있는 'pair work' 입니다. 단어와 구문의 경우
되도록 스님들의 환경에 맞는 것으로 수록하여 더욱
효과적인 학습을 기하였습니다. 'pair work' 에서는
밑줄 친 부분을 다른 단어로 대체하여 동일한 문장을
지루함 없이 자연스럽게 암기가 가능하도록 하였습
니다.

One-Line Expressions 한 줄 표현

회화부의 마지막에 수록하여 자주 쓰이는 말과 표현
을 쉽게 익히도록 했습니다. 예문을 반복해서 연습하
여 일상에서 자연스럽게 사용할 수 있도록, 내것으로
만드세요.

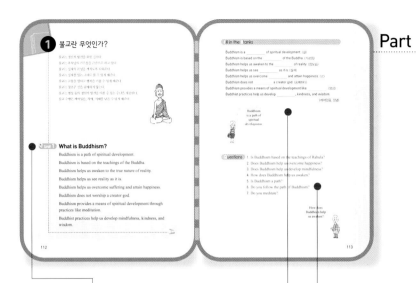

Part ②

Unit

각 주제에 해당하는 설명

2부 〈불교 교리〉와 3부 〈한국 불교의 역사와 문화〉에서는 기본적으로 알아야 할 주제를 선정하여 먼저 한글 지문, 그에 해당하는 영어 지문을 실었습니다.

Fill in the Blanks
빈칸 넣기

본문의 주요 부분을 발췌하여 빈칸에 알맞은 단어를 찾아 넣도록 하였습니다. 이는 방금 배운 본문을 복습하는 동시에 주요 단어를 한 번 써보며 다시 익히도록 한 것입니다.

Questions 질문

본문에서 배운 내용에 대한 질문을 주고받는 상황입니다. 이 부분은 학생들끼리 연습해도 되고 또는 선생님과 학생이 질문을 주고받아도 됩니다. 핵심 패턴을 익혀 그 의미를 확실하게 전달할 수 있도록 하세요.

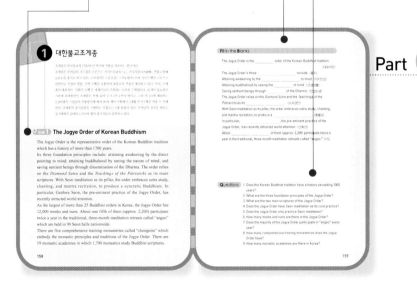

Part ③

Contents

Part 3 The History and Culture of Korean Buddhism 한국불교의 역사와 문화

Part 1

English Conversation
영어 회화

1 템플스테이

마틴: 안녕하세요?
스님: 안녕하세요?
마틴: 여기가 조계사인가요?
스님: 네, 여기가 조계사입니다.
　　　어디서 오셨나요?
마틴: 저는 미국에서 왔습니다.
　　　템플스테이에 참가하기 위해서요.
스님: 아, 그러세요. 잘 오셨습니다.

Unit 1 **Templestay**

Martin: Hello!

Monk: Hi! Can I help you?

Martin: Is this Jogye-sa Temple?

Monk: Yes, it is.

Where are you from?

Martin: I'm from America.

I'm here to participate in the Templestay program.

Monk: Great! Welcome to Jogye-sa!

▶ '여기가 ~인가요?'를 물어볼 때엔 보통 '**Is this ~?**'를 사용한다.

여기가 대각사인가요? Is this Daegak-sa Temple?

여기가 시청인가요? Is this the City Hall?

여기가 기획부인가요? Is this the planning department?

여기가 어디인가요? Where are we? (Where am I?)

여기가 몇 층인가요? What floor are we on? (What floor is this?)

▶ '참가하다'라는 의미의 '**participate in**'은 꼭 '**in**'과 함께 사용한다.

새 프로젝트에 참가하다. participate in the new project

템플스테이 참가자 Templestay participants

시합에 참가하다. enter a competition (contest)

> Is this
> Daegak-sa
> Temple?

Pair **W**ork Practice by substituting the underlined words with other proper words and phrases.

Martin: Is this Daeheung-sa Temple?

Monk: Yes, it is.

Where are you from?

Martin: I'm from Canada.

I'm here to participate in the Summer Dharma Camp.

Monk: Great! Welcome to Daeheung-sa!

> Where
> are you from?

2 첫 인사

스님: 처음 뵙겠습니다.

잭슨: 만나서 반갑습니다.

스님: 이름이 어떻게 됩니까?

잭슨: 제 이름은 잭슨입니다.

스님: 네, 말씀 많이 들었습니다. 만나보고 싶었습니다.

잭슨: 성함을 어찌 불러야 할까요?

스님: 제 이름은 수월입니다. 하지만 그냥 스님으로 부르세요.
　　　한국에서는 모든 남자 여자 스님들을 '스님'으로 부릅니다.

잭슨: 그렇군요. 감사합니다, '스님'.

Unit 2 First Greetings

Sunim:　Hello, nice to meet you.

Jackson:　Nice to meet you, too.

Sunim:　What's your name?

Jackson:　I'm Jackson.

Sunim:　Oh! I've heard a lot about you.

I've been looking forward to meeting you.

Jackson:　How may I call you?

Sunim:　My Dharma name is Suwol. But you can just call me Sunim. All monks and nuns are called Sunim in the Korean tradition.

Jackson:　I see. Thank you, Sunim.

▶ ~ 에 대해 말씀 많이 들었습니다. **I've heard a lot about~.**

그 남자(여자)에 대해 말씀 많이 들었습니다. I've heard a lot about him/her.

그 이야기 많이 들었습니다. I've heard a lot about the story.

그 절에 대해 많이 들었습니다. I've heard a lot about the temple.

▶ ~ 를 - 고대하다, 매우~하고 싶다. (과거부터 현재까지 이어질 때: 현재완료진행)

have been looking forward to 동사 원형 + **ing**(동명사)

그 영화가 매우 보고 싶었습니다. I've been looking forward to watching the movie.

그 절에 너무 가고 싶었습니다. I've been looking forward to going to the temple.

▶ 당신을 어떻게 부르면 됩니까? **How may I address you?**

　　　　　　　　　　　　　　　By what name should I call you?

(위치가 높거나 공경해야 할 사람의 이름, 특별한 호칭을 쓰는 분을 부르고자 할 때)

나는 그 여자를 어떻게 불러야 할까요? How may I address her?

나는 당신 어머니를 어떻게 불러야 할까요? By what name should I call your mother?

나는 당신 은사를 어떻게 불러야 합니까? How may I address your master?

그냥 주지스님이라고 부르시면 됩니다. You can just call him Juji Sunim.

▶ 법명 **Dharma name, Buddhist name**

제 법명은 수월입니다. My Buddhist name is Suwol.

I'm Jackson.

Pair Work Practice by substituting the underlined words with other proper words and phrases.

Sunim: I've heard a lot about you, Anna.

　　　　I've been looking forward to meeting you.

Anna: How should I address you?

Sunim: My Dharma name is Bohaeng. But you can just call me Sunim.

Anna: I see. See you later Sunim.

3 참가신청서 작성

스님: 저는 템플스테이 담당자입니다.
　　　해인사에 오신 것을 환영합니다.
애나: 절이 정말 아름답군요.
　　　저는 한국불교에 관심이 많습니다.
스님: 해인사는 한국불교의 대표적인 사찰이지요.
　　　이 양식을 작성해주시겠습니까?
애나: 네, 여기 쓰면 되나요?
스님: 네.

Unit 3 Filling Out a Form

Sunim: I'm in charge of the Templestay.

Welcome to Haein-sa Temple.

Anna: It's a really beautiful temple here.

I'm very interested in Korean Buddhism.

Sunim: Haein-sa Temple is one of the most outstanding temples in Korean Buddhism.

Would you please fill out this form?

Anna: Sure! Should I fill it out here?

Sunim: Yes.

▶ 저는 ~ 담당(자)입니다. **I'm in charge of** (대)명사/동명사.

저는 외국인 방문객 안내 담당입니다. I'm in charge of guiding foreign visitors.

저는 한국불교문화 홍보 담당입니다. I'm in charge of promoting Korean Buddhism and Culture.

▶ 이 사찰은 정말 아름답군요. **It's a really beautiful temple here.**

이곳은 정말 어둡군요. It's really dark here.

이곳은 정말 밝군요. It's really bright here.

이곳은 정말 따뜻하군요. It's really warm here.

▶ 저는 ~에 관심이 있습니다. **I'm interested in** (대)명사/동명사.

저는 한국문화에 관심이 있습니다. I'm interested in Korean culture.

저는 한국 선불교에 관심이 많습니다. I'm very interested in Korean Seon Buddhism.

▶ 양식(서식)을 작성하다. **fill out a form**

▶ 제가 ~을 해야 할까요? **Should I** 동사?

제가 그곳에 가야 할까요? Should I go there?

제가 조계사에 가야 할까요? Should I go to Jogye-sa temple?

제가 학교에 가야 할까요? Should I go to school?

▶ ~을 해주시겠습니까? **Would you please** 동사?

내일 절에 오실 수 있겠습니까? Would you please come to the temple tomorrow?

시간 좀 지켜주실 수 있습니까? Would you please be on time?

제가 가도록 허락해주실 수 있습니까? Would you please let me go?

Pair Work Practice by substituting the underlined words with other proper words and phrases.

Sunim: I'm in charge of Dharma Propagation.
        Welcome to Tongdo-sa Temple.

Anna: It's a really old temple here. I'm very interested in
        Korean Buddhist history.

Sunim: Tongdo-sa Temple is one of the most historic temples
        in Korea. Would you please visit our Buddhist
        Museum, too?

Anna: Sure!

4 방 안내

스님: 조계사 템플스테이에 오신 것을 환영합니다.

마틴: 만나서 반갑습니다.

스님: 네, 반갑습니다. 그럼 방을 안내해 드리겠습니다. 저를 따라오세요.

마틴: 네.

스님: 이 방의 이름은 연화실이라고 합니다.
　　　앞으로 3박4일 동안 마틴이 머물 방입니다.

마틴: 아, 네~ 너무 멋져요.

스님: 우선 짐을 풀고 잠시 쉬었다가 30분 후에 만나요. 데리러 오겠습니다.

마틴: 네, 감사합니다. 나중에 만나요.

Unit 4 Showing a Participant to the Guest Room

Sunim: Welcome to the Templestay at Jogye-sa Temple.

Martin: Nice to meet you.

Sunim: Nice to meet you, too. Let me show you to your room.
Please follow me.

Martin: OK.

Sunim: The name of this room is "Yeon-hwa room." It means
"lotus flower room." You will stay in this room for
four days and three nights.

Martin: Wow~! I see. It's great.

Sunim: Please unpack your bag and take a rest first. I'll come
back for you in 30 minutes.

Martin: OK. Thank you. See you soon.

▶ **Let me show you to** + 명사(구) 안내하다.

법당으로 안내하겠습니다. Let me show him (to) the Dharma hall.

▶ **Let me show you** + 명사(구) 보여주다.

제가 그에게 절하는 법을 보여주겠습니다. Let me show him how to prostrate.

목탁을 보여 드리겠습니다. Let me show you the moktak, or the wooden handbell.

▶ 저를 따라오세요. **Please follow me.**

저 스님을 따라가십시오. Please follow that Sunim.

▶ 그 뜻은 ~ 입니다. **It means** 명사/명사구/동명사.

그 뜻은 '조용히 해야 한다' 는 뜻입니다. It means 'keeping silence'.

그것은 깨달음이란 뜻입니다. It means enlightenment.

▶ ~(시간) 내에 돌아올 것이다. 주어 **will come back in** 시간.

제가 1시간 후에 돌아올 것입니다. I will come back in 1 hour.

그가 10분 후면 돌아올 것입니다. He will come back in 10 minutes.

▶ 짐을 풀다. **unpack**

우선 여행 가방의 짐을 먼저 푸세요. Please unpack your suitcase first.

우선 소포를 먼저 푸세요. Please unpack your parcel first.

우선 장바구니를 먼저 푸세요. Please unpack your groceries first.

The name of this
room is "Yeon-hwa
room." It means
"lotus flower room."

Pair **W**ork Free Response

1. Can you show me around the temple?

2. What's the name of this building?

3. Did you pack your suitcase yourself?

4. When will the Sunim be back to the temple?

5. Will she be back by 7 pm?

5 템플스테이 신청

잭슨: 템플스테이에 참여하려면 어떻게 신청해야 할까요?

스님: 먼저 템플스테이 홈페이지에서 가고 싶은 사찰의 일정을 확인하세요.

잭슨: 인터넷으로 신청이 가능하나요?

스님: 그럼요, 다국어로 되어 있어서 인터넷으로도 신청이 가능하죠.
　　　템플스테이 사무국으로 전화해서 안내를 받으셔도 됩니다.

잭슨: 템플스테이 홈페이지 주소는 어떻게 되나요?

스님: http://eng.templestay.com

잭슨: 어떤 언어들이 가능한가요?

스님: 영어, 일어, 중국어, 독일어, 프랑스어, 스페인어 등 총 6개 국어가 가능해요.

잭슨: 그렇군요. 감사합니다.

Unit 5 Applying for a Templestay

Jackson: How can I apply for the Templestay program?

Sunim: You should check out the Templestay website on the Internet. There you will find temples that offer templestays and the schedule.

Jackson: Can I apply online?

Sunim: Sure. There is a multiple language service on the website so that you can apply online. Or you could call the office directly to get information.

Jackson: What's the address of the website?

Sunim: http://eng.templestay.com

Jackson: What languages are used?

Sunim: English, Japanese, Chinese, German, French and Spanish; six languages in total.

Jackson: I see. Thank you.

Words & Phrases

▶ ~을 어떻게 지원(신청)해야 하나요?

How can I apply for ~? (특정 직업, 지위나 프로그램에 지원할 때)

How can I apply to ~? (기관, 단체, 사람 등에 지원할 때)

장학금을 어떻게 신청해야 하나요? How can I apply for the scholarship?

어떻게 그 절의 자원봉사자로 지원해야 하나요? How can I apply for a volunteer position at the temple?

▶ 자동차 대출을 신청하다. **apply for a car loan**

나는 대출과에 자동차 대출을 신청했다. I applied to the loan department for a car loan.

중앙승가대학에 어떻게 지원해야 하나요? How can I apply to Jung-Ang Sangha University?

▶ ~을 확인해 보셔야 합니다. **You should check out ~**

그 정보는 교육원에서 확인해 보셔야 합니다. You should check out the information from the Bureau of Monastic Training.

▶ ~한 결과 ~하다.

그곳에 차가 너무 막혀서 걸어가야 했다. There was too much traffic so we had to walk.

눈이 몹시 많이 내려서 대관령 주위의 모든 길이 통제되었다. There was too much snow so all the roads were closed around Daegwallyeong.

Pair Work Practice by substituting the underlined words with other proper words and phrases.

Jackson: How can I apply for the scholarship program?

Sunim: You should check out the information on the Internet. There you will find the details.

Jackson: Can I apply online?

Sunim: Sure. There are English and Korean language services on the website so that you can apply online.

Jackson: I see. Thank you.

6 사찰 찾아가기

스님: 마틴은 오늘까지 조계사에 머문다고 했죠?

마틴: 네.

스님: 그럼 어디로 가나요?

마틴: 범어사를 찾아가려고 합니다. 그런데 가는 방법을 잘 모르겠어요.

스님: 기차를 이용하면 편해요. 서울역에서 KTX를 타고 부산역으로 가세요.

마틴: 부산역에 내린 다음에는요?

스님: 부산역에서 범어사 가는 전철이나 택시를 이용하면 됩니다.
　　　버스 노선까지는 제가 잘 모르겠어요.

마틴: 아뇨. 그 정도면 충분해요. 정말 감사합니다.

스님: 다음에 또 만나요.

Unit 6　Finding Your Way to the Temple

Sunim: Martin! Did you say that you're going to stay at Jogye-sa until today?

Martin: Yes.

Sunim: Then where are you going to next?

Martin: I want to visit Beomeo-sa Temple, but I don't know how to get there.

Sunim: It's easy to get there by train. Take a KTX train from Seoul station to Busan.

Martin: What do I do when I get off the train at Busan station?

Sunim: You can take a taxi or subway going towards Beomeo-sa Temple, but I'm not sure about the bus line.

Martin: That's okay, that's enough. Thank you so much.

Sunim: See you again.

▶ (당신이) ～ 한다고 말했나요? **Did you say that you're going to ~?**

내일 월정사에 간다고 말했습니까? Did you say that you're going to visit Woljeong-sa Temple tomorrow?

다음 주에 성지순례 간다고 했습니까? Did you say that you're going to go on a pilgrimage next week?

내년에 승가대학교에 지원할 거라고 했습니까? Did you say that you're going to apply to a monastic academy next year?

▶ 저는 ～에 가고 싶습니다. **I want to visit** 장소

저는 태화산 마곡사에 가고 싶습니다. I want to visit Magok-sa Temple on Taehwa Mountain.

저는 해인사에 가서 팔만대장경을 보고 싶습니다. I want to visit Haein-sa temple to see the *Tripitaka Koreana*.

▶ **how to get to** 구체적인 장소 ～에 어떻게 가는지

조계사에 어떻게 가는지 모르겠어요. I don't know how to get to Jogye-sa Temple.

인천공항에 어떻게 가는지 모르겠어요. I don't know how to get to Incheon Airport.

▶ **by +** 운송 수단

그곳에 가려면 택시(기차, 버스)를 타고 가는 게 쉬워요. It's easy to get there by taxi (train, bus).

그곳에 가려면 걸어가는 게 편합니다. It's easy to get there on foot.

▶ ～에 내리면 어떻게 해야 하나요?

서울역에 내리면 그 다음엔 어떻게 해야 하나요? What do I do when I get off the train at Seoul station?

인사동 전철역에 내리면 그 다음엔 어떻게 해야 하나요? What do I do when I get off the subway at Insadong?

고속버스터미널에 버스를 타고 내리면 그 다음엔 어떻게 해야 하나요? What do I do when I get off the bus at the express bus terminal?

Pair Work Practice by substituting the underlined words with other proper words and phrases.

Sunim: Martin! Did you say that you're going to leave today?

Martin: Yes.

Sunim: Then where are you going to next?

Martin: I want to visit Woljeong-sa Temple. But I don't know how to get there.

Sunim: It's easy to get there by express bus. Take an express bus from Seoul to Jinbu bus terminal.

기상 시간

스님: 내일 새벽 3시에 법당에서 예불이 있습니다.
　　　2시 40분에 일어날 예정입니다.

애나: (깜짝 놀라며) 새벽 2시 40분이요?
　　　스님들은 평소에도 그 시간에 일어나나요?

스님: 네. 일찍 일어나서 새벽 예불 올릴 준비를 합니다.

애나: 한국 사찰에서는 다 이렇게 일찍 일어나나요?

스님: 네, 그런 편이지요. 보통은 3시에 하지만, 도시에서는 새벽 4시에 예불을 하는
　　　곳도 있고, 5시에 예불하는 곳도 있습니다.

애나: (깜짝 놀라며) 그럼 잠은 언제 자나요?

스님: (빙긋이 웃으며) 저녁 9~10시쯤에는 잠자리에 듭니다.

Unit 7 Wake-up Time

Sunim: There is an early morning ceremony at 3 am in the
　　　　Dharma hall, so you should wake up at 2:40 am.

Anna: (Surprised) At 2:40 am? Do all monks and nuns wake
　　　　up at that time, too?

Sunim: Yes. They must wake up early to prepare for the
　　　　morning ceremony.

Anna: Do all monks and nuns generally wake up as early as
　　　　that?

Sunim: Yes, usually. The morning ceremony starts at 3 am in
　　　　general, but some temples in the cities start at 4 am or
　　　　5 am.

Anna: (Surprised) When do they go to bed?

Sunim: (Smiling) They go to bed between 9 and 10 pm.

▶ 당신은 ~ (시간)에 일어나야 합니다. **You should get up at** 시간.

당신은 동틀 무렵에 일어나야 합니다. You should get up at dawn.

당신은 내일 아침 7시에 일어나야 합니다. You should get up at 7 in the morning tomorrow.

그는 매일 새벽 4시에 일어나야 합니다. He should get up at 4 am everyday.

당신도 동틀 무렵에 일어납니까? Do you get up at dawn, too?

스님들도 새벽 두 시 반에 일어납니까? Do sunims get up at 2:30 am, too?

▶ ~는 언제 일어납니까? **When do/does** 주어 **get up?**

당신은 몇 시에 일어납니까? When do you get up?

그 스님은 몇 시에 일어납니까? When does that sunim get up?

▶ 일반적으로 **generally / usually / in general**

▶ 새벽 예불 **early morning ceremony**

▶ ~ 시에 **at ~** / ~ 쯤에 **around ~** / 대략적인 시간 범위(~에서 ~사이) **between ~ and ~**

저는 자정쯤에 잠자리에 듭니다. I go to bed around midnight.

저는 주로 저녁 여덟 시에서 아홉 시 사이에 잠자리에 듭니다. I usually go to bed between 8 and 9 pm.

You should wake up at 2:40 am.

Free Response.

1. Do you wake up early?
2. What time do you wake up?
3. What time do you go to the refectory for breakfast?
4. Did you go to bed late last night?
5. Do monks and nuns sometimes sleep late?
6. Can you keep the lights on after the official bedtime at temples?

Chapter 2 Showing a Guest around the Temple 사찰 안내

1 법당

스님: 우리 절에 잘 오셨습니다.

절에는 처음인가요?

마틴: 네. 절에는 처음입니다.

스님: 여기는 조계사라고 합니다.

그리고 이곳은 법당입니다.

마틴: 법당에서는 무엇을 하나요?

스님: 법당은 스님들이 모여서 불교의식을 행하는 곳입니다.

마틴: 아, 그렇군요.

Unit 1 Dharma Hall

Sunim: Welcome to our temple.

Is this your first time visiting a temple?

Martin: Yes, this is my first time.

Sunim: This is Jogye-sa Temple.

And this is the Dharma hall.

Martin: What do you do in a Dharma hall?

Sunim: It's a place all monks and nuns gather to have Buddhist ceremonies.

Martin: Oh, I see.

▶ 이번이 처음인가요? **Is this your first time visiting** <u>장소</u>?

한국을 방문한 것은 이번이 처음인가요? Is this your first time visiting Korea?

사리탑을 본 것은 이번이 처음인가요? Is this your first time seeing a reliquary pagoda?

비로전에는 이번에 처음 와보나요? Is this your first time coming into the Hall of Vairocana?

연등은 이번에 처음 만들어보나요? Is this your first time making a lotus lantern?

참선은 이번에 처음 해보나요? Is this your first time doing Seon meditation?

▶ 그곳에서 무엇을 하나요? **What do you do in** <u>장소</u>?

그것을 무엇에 활용합니까? What do you do with <u>물건</u>?

대웅전에서는 무엇을 합니까? What do you do in the Main Buddha Hall?

목탁은 무슨 용도로 쓰나요? What do you use the wooden handbell for?

▶ ~을 하기 위해 모이다. **gather to** <u>(동사 원형)</u>

매년 사월 초파일에는 많은 불자들이 연등을 켜기 위해 절에 온다.

A lot of Buddhists gather to hang lotus lanterns at temples on the Buddha's Birthday every year.

어린이들이 부처님께 절을 드리려고 모였다. The children gathered to prostrate to the Buddha.

It's a place all monks and nuns gather to have Buddhist ceremonies.

Free Response

1. What do you do in the Main Buddha Hall?
2. What do you do in the Seon Hall?
3. What do you do with the moktak?
4. What do you do with candles and incense?
5. Is this your first time visiting Korea?
6. Is this your first time participating in the Templestay?

2 대웅전

스님: 이쪽으로 따라오세요.

마틴: 여기가 어딘가요?

스님: 여기는 대웅전입니다. 석가모니 부처님을 모신
곳이랍니다. 신발을 벗고 오른쪽 문으로 들어오세요. 한국 절에서는 일반 신도
님들은 법당의 오른쪽 문으로 들어오고, 스님들은 가운데문으로 들어온답니다.

마틴: 예, 알겠습니다. 아… 부처님이 여러 분 계시네요.

스님: 네, 가운데 부처님은 석가모니불이고요,
왼쪽은 관세음보살, 오른쪽은 대세지보살입니다.

마틴: 아, 그렇군요.

Unit 2 Main Buddha Hall

Sunim: Follow me this way.

Martin: What is this place?

Sunim: This is the Main Buddha Hall. A statue of Sakyamuni
Buddha is here. Please take off your shoes and come
into the right hand door. In Korean temples, laypeople
enter the Main Buddha Hall through the door on the
right side of the building, and monks and nuns enter
through the front central door.

Martin: I see. Oh... there are many Buddha statues.

Sunim: Yes, Sakyamuni Buddha is in the middle,
Avalokitesvara Bodhisattva (Boddhisattva of
Compassion) is on the left and Mahasthamaprapta
Bodhisattva (Bodhisattva of Power) is on the right.

Martin: I see.

▶ 이곳은 ~입니다. **This is 명사.**

이곳은 종무소입니다. This is the temple office.

이곳은 산신각입니다. Here is *Sansingak* (the Mountain God Shrine).

여기는 암자입니다. This is a hermitage.

▶ ~을 벗으세요. **Please take off ~.**

장갑을 벗으세요. Please take off your gloves.

절을 할 땐 모자를 벗으세요. Please take off your hat when you prostrate.

▶ 석가모니불 **Sakyamuni Buddha**

▶ 관세음보살 **Avalokitesvara Bodhisattva**

▶ 대세지보살 **Mahasthamaprapta Bodhisattva (Bodhisattva of Power)**

▶ 일반신도들 **laypeople, lay Buddhists**

▶ 오른쪽 문 **the door on the right side of the building**

▶ 중앙문 **the front central door (the central door at the front)**

※ 중앙에 at the center (of ~) / ※ ~ 앞에 in front of ~

This is the Main
Buddha Hall.

Oh... there are
many Buddha
statues.

Pair Work   Free Response

1. Which way is the temple office?

2. How can I get to the Main Buddha Hall?

3. How many affiliated hermitages does this temple have?

4. Should I take off my hat when paying homage to the Buddha?

5. Can lay Buddhists enter the Dharma hall through the front central doors?

3 범종루

잭슨: 이곳은 무엇을 하는 곳인가요?

스님: 여기는 범종루입니다. 종각이라고도 하지요.

잭슨: (사물을 가리키며) 이것들은 다 뭐죠?

스님: 이것은 대종, 이것은 목어, 이것은 운판, 이것은 법고랍니다.

잭슨: 이것을 치는 것도 다 의미가 있나요?

스님: 네. 대종은 지옥중생을 위해 울리고요, 법고는 축생을 위해서 칩니다.
     그리고 목어는 물고기를 위해서, 운판은 새들을 위해서 치지요.

잭슨: 네, 잘 알겠습니다.

Unit 3 Bell Pavilion

Jackson: What is this place for?

Sunim: This is the Bell Pavilion. It's also called the Bell Tower.

Jackson: (Pointing at objects) What are these?

Sunim: This is the Buddhist bell, and this is the wooden fish; that's the cloud-shaped gong, and that is the Dharma drum.

Jackson: When you sound them, does it mean anything?

Sunim: Yes, it does. The Buddhist bell is sounded for all sentient beings suffering from the hell-like world. The Dharma drum is sounded for animals. The Wooden fish is for fish; and the cloud-shaped gong for birds.

Jackson: I got it.

Words & Phrases

▶ 이곳은 무엇을 하는 곳입니까? **What is this place for?**

▶ 이곳은 ~라고도 불립니다. **This is also called** <u>이름</u>.

이곳은 삼성각이라고도 불립니다. This is also called *Samseonggak*.

이곳은 해우소라고도 불립니다. This is also called *Haeuso*.

▶ 악기는 ~을 위해 연주됩니다.

그 음악은 평화를 위해 연주되었습니다. The music was played for peace.

그 종은 새해를 맞이하기 위해 울렸습니다. The bell was rung to celebrate a new year.

▶ 어떤 의미가 있는가요?

목탁은 무슨 의미로 칩니까? When you hit a/the *moktak*, are there any meanings?

성지순례를 하는 것은 무슨 의미가 있는가요? When you go on a pilgrimage, is there any meaning?

▶ 일체중생 **all sentient beings**

▶ 축생(들) **animal(s)**

▶ 그렇군요, 알겠어요. **I got it.**

> What is this place for?

Pair Work Practice by substituting the underlined words with other proper words and phrases.

Jackson: What is this place for?

Sunim: This is <u>the Mountain God Shrine</u>. It's also called <u>*Sansingak*</u>.

Jackson: When you get in the hall, are there any meanings?

Sunim: Of course. This shrine is for <u>protecting and respecting the Mountain God</u> of the temple.

Jackson: I got it.

31

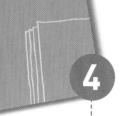

4 각단

(스님을 따라 각단을 돌고 있다. 관음전에서)

잭슨: 여기에도 불상이 있네요? 이 분은 누구신가요?

스님: 여기는 관음전이라고 하고, 이 분은 관세음보살님이십니다.

잭슨: 그럼 저곳과 저기도 각각 다른 분이 계신가요?

스님: 네. 그래요. 여기저기 있는 법당에는 각각 다른 분들이 모셔져 있습니다.

잭슨: 그렇군요. 저기는 어느 분이 모셔져 있나요?

스님: 저기는 지장전이고, 지장보살님이 모셔져 있습니다.

Unit 4 Various Dharma Halls

(Following a monk around various Dharma halls. At the Hall of Avalokitesvara)

Jackson: There is also a Buddha statue here. Who's this?

Sunim: It's the Hall of Avalokitesvara and this statue is Avalokitesvara Bodhisattva.

Jackson: Then, are there some other Buddha statues inside that hall and that hall over there?

Sunim: Yes. You're right. There are different Buddha statues in each Dharma hall.

Jackson: I see. What kind of Buddha statue is inside that Dharma hall?

Sunim: That place is the Hall of Ksitigarbha, so there is the statue of Ksitigarbha Bodhisattva (Earth-Storehouse Bodhisattva).

▶ ～이 있다. **There is ~ / There are ~**

이 절에도 석탑이 있네요. There is a stone pagoda at this temple, too.

여기에도 염주가 있네요. There are prayer beads here too.

▶ 의문문에 쓰이는 **some**과 **any**

있다고 가정하고 물을 때 **some** / 없다고 가정하고 물을 때 **any**

문제가 좀 있나요? Are there some other problems?

아무 문제 없나요? Is there any problem?

아침공양이 아직 좀 남아 있나요? Is there some more breakfast left?

아침공양이 남은 게 아무것도 없나요? Is there any more breakfast left?

법당에 신도님들이 아직 좀 계신가요? Are there some other people in the Dharma hall?

법당에는 신도님이 아무도 없나요? Are there any people in the Dharma hall?

▶ 지장전 **Hall of Ksitigarbha (Bodhisattva)**

▶ 지장보살상 **the statue of Ksitigarbha Bodhisattva**

Pair Work Practice by substituting the underlined words with other proper words and phrases.

Jackson: There also is a Buddha statue. Who's this?

Sunim:　It's the Hall of the Future Buddha and this statue is Maitreya Buddha.

Jackson: Then, are there some other Buddha statues inside that Hall too?

Sunim:　Yes. There are different Buddha statues in each Dharma hall.

Jackson: I see. What kind of Buddha statue is inside that Dharma hall?

Sunim:　That place is *Birojeon* (the Hall of the Cosmic Buddha), so there is the statue of Vairocana Buddha.

5 부도

스님: 여기는 부도입니다.

애나: 이것도 탑인가요? 다른 탑과는 모양이 다른데요.

스님: 부도도 탑입니다. 스님들의 사리나 유골을 모신 탑을 부도라고 한답니다.

애나: 부도는 이 사찰에만 있나요?

스님: 아니요. 다른 사찰에도 있습니다. 사찰 뒤쪽이나 그 주변에 살펴보면 많이 있습니다.

애나: 모든 스님들이 열반하시면 다 부도를 만드나요?

스님: 아니요. 그 사찰에 머무셨던 스님 중에서 덕이 높은 큰스님만을 기려서 만든답니다.

애나: 그럼, 스님도 나중에 열반에 드시면 부도를 만드나요?

스님: (머리를 긁적이며 웃으면서) 글쎄요.

Unit 5 Memorial Stupa

Sunim: This is a memorial stupa.

Anna: Is this a pagoda as well? It looks different from other pagodas.

Sunim: The memorial stupa is also a pagoda. It is called a memorial stupa because this is a stupa that holds the relics and ashes of monks.

Anna: Is the memorial stupa only at this temple?

Sunim: No, other temples have them as well. There are many if you look for them in the backyards or surroundings of temples.

Anna: Do all monks and nuns get a memorial stupa after they pass away?

Sunim: No. Only if they were an enlightened or outstandingly compassionate monk or nun who lived at the temple.

Anna: So are you going to get a memorial stupa after you pass away?

Sunim: (Scratching his head and smiling) Well... not sure.

Words & Phrases

▶ **~와 다르게 보인다. It looks different from ~.**

그 절은 다른 절과 좀 달라보이는군요. This temple looks different from other temples.

한국불교는 티베트불교와 좀 다르군요. Korean Buddhism looks different from Tibetan Buddhism.

▶ **~이라 불리다(~라고 하다). It is called ~.**

그것은 합장주라고 한다. It is called a *Hapjangju*.

그것은 관세음보살님이라고 한다. It is called Avalokitesvara Bodhisattva.

그는 스님이라고 불린다. He is called Sunim.

▶ **~해야만(비로소), ~의 경우에만 only if ~**

영어 시험에 합격해야만 그 학교에 갈 수 있습니다. You can enter the school only if you pass the English test.

스님이 되어야만 그 절에서 수행할 수 있습니다. You can practice in that temple only if you become a monk.

▶ **~할 예정입니까? be going to ~?**

당신은 내일 아침 일찍 떠날 예정입니까? Are you going to leave early in the morning tomorrow?

당신은 인도로 여행을 갈 예정입니까? Are you going to travel to India?

당신은 반야심경을 염송할 예정입니까? Are you going to chant the *Heart Sutra*?

저는 인도로 여행을 갈 예정입니다. I'm going to travel to India.

저는 반야심경을 독송할 예정입니다. I'm going to chant the *Heart Sutra*.

▶ 사리와 유골 **relics and ashes**   ▶ 사찰 주변 **surroundings of temples**

▶ 부도 **a memorial stupa**   ▶ 돌아가시다 **pass away**

▶ 뒷마당 **backyards**   ▶ 주변 **surroundings**

Pair Work Practice by substituting the underlined words with other proper words and phrases.

Sunim: This is a memorial stupa.

Anna: Whose memorial stupa is it?

Sunim: It belongs to Master Samyeong, a great monk of the Joseon Dynasty.

Anna: Did he reside in this temple?

Sunim: I think so.

Anna: It looks pretty old. Is it older than the stone lantern?

Sunim: Well, I'm not sure.

 야보송

당당한 대도여! 밝고 분명하도다.

사람마다 본래 갖추고 있고, 저마다 다 이뤄져 있네.

《금강경오가해(金剛經五家解)》〈야보송(冶父頌)〉

The majestic Great Way is bright and clear.
Everyone is originally endowed with it, and each
one has already attained it.

- Verses by Yabo

6 삼보사찰

스님: 한국에는 삼보사찰이 있습니다.

애나: 삼보사찰이 뭡니까?

스님: 먼저 삼보가 무엇인지 설명해 드리겠습니다.

　　　삼보란 부처님과 부처님의 가르침, 그리고 스님들을 가리키는 말입니다.

　　　이것을 상징적으로 세 군데 사찰로 선정한 것입니다.

애나: 그 세 곳은 어디인가요?

스님: 불보사찰로는 통도사, 법보사찰로는 해인사, 승보사찰은 송광사입니다.

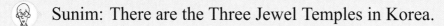 **Unit 6** **The Three Jewel Temples**

Sunim: There are the Three Jewel Temples in Korea.

Anna: What are the Three Jewel Temples?

Sunim: First I will tell you what the Three Jewels are. It means the Buddha, the Dharma, which are the Buddha's teachings, and the Sangha, which is the monastic community of Buddhist monks and nuns. So there are three symbolic monasteries for the Three Jewels.

Anna: What are the three temples?

Sunim: The Buddha Jewel Temple is Tongdo-sa; the Dharma Jewel Temple is Haein-sa; and the Sangha Jewel Temple is Songgwang-sa.

▶ ~에 대해 이야기해줄 것이다.

제가 당신이 지금 보고 있는 것에 대해 이야기해 드리겠습니다. I'll tell you what you're looking at right now.

저 행자님이 당신이 무엇을 해야할지 말해줄 겁니다. The postulant will tell you what you should do.

▶ ~는 무슨 의미인가요? **What does 명사/대명사 mean?**

발우공양은 어떤 의미인가요? What does *baru gongyang* mean?

공안은 뜻이 무엇인가요? What does *gongan* mean?

해우소라는 말은 무슨 뜻이죠? What does *hae-uso* mean?

▶ 그 의미는 ~, 즉 ~ 이라는 것이다. **It means ~, which 동사 + 명사.**

그 의미는 평화, 즉 전쟁이 없는 것을 의미합니다. It means peace, which has no war.

그 의미는 자비심, 즉 완전한 사랑을 보여줌을 의미합니다. It means compassion, which shows the complete love.

▶ 승가 **the monastic community of Buddhist monks and nuns**

▶ 삼보사찰 **the Three Jewel Temples/Monasteries**

▶ 불보사찰 **the Buddha Jewel Temple**

▶ 법보사찰 **the Dharma Jewel Temple**

▶ 승보사찰 **the Sangha Jewel Temple**

Pair Work Practice by substituting the underlined words with the proper words and phrases.

Sunim: There are Three Avalokitesvara Temples in Korea.

Anna: What are they?

Sunim: People go there to offer prayers to Avalokitesvara Bodhisattva.

They are Bori-am Hermitage, Naksan-sa Temple and Bomun-sa Temple.

Anna: Have you been to any one of them?

Sunim: I've been to Bori-am. It looks over the South Sea.

Anna: It must be beautiful!

해우소

마틴: (배를 움켜쥐고) 화장실을 가고 싶은데 어디로 가면 되죠?

스님: 문을 열고 나가서 오른쪽으로 돌면 바로 나옵니다.

스님: (화장실에 다녀온 후) 마틴, 어디 아파요?

마틴: 한국에 온 지 3일이 되었는데, 배가 자주 아파요.

스님: 물이 바뀌어서 그런가 봅니다. 끓인 물을 마시는 게 좋겠습니다.

마틴: 네, 알겠어요. 그런데 화장실에 알 수 없는 이름이 쓰여 있던데요?

스님: 사찰에서는 화장실을 '해우소' 라고 합니다.

마틴: 무슨 뜻이죠?

스님: 근심을 푼다는 뜻입니다.

마틴: (웃으며) 재밌네요. 듣고 보니 정말 근심이 풀리는 것 같아요.

Unit 7 "Haeuso" (Restroom)

Martin: (Holding his tummy) I need to go to the restroom. Where is it?

Sunim: When you get out the door, make a right turn then you will see it right away.

Sunim: (After seeing him come back from the restroom) Martin, what's the problem?

Martin: It's been three days since I arrived in Korea, but I've often had a stomachache.

Sunim: It might be due to the different water here. It would be better for you to drink boiled water.

Martin: All right. I'll do that. By the way, I saw an unfamiliar building name on the restroom.

Sunim: Restrooms are called "Haeuso" in Korean temples.

Martin: What does that mean?

 Sunim: It means it releases worries.

 Martin: (Laughing) Interesting! It sounds like it already
released my worries.

Words & Phrases

▶ ~ 해야 해요. **I need to ~.**

나는 수행을 더 열심히 해야 해요. I need to practice harder.

나는 강원에 가야 해요. I need to go to the monastic school.

나는 108배를 해야 해요. I need to do 108 prostrations.

▶ 그러면 **then**

새벽예불에 일어날 때 알람시계를 사용하세요. 그러면 일찍 일어날 수 있을 것입니다.
When you wake up early in the morning for the morning ceremony, use the alarm clock. Then you will wake up early.

법당을 나갈 때, 염주를 제자리에 갖다놓으세요. 그래야 다른 사람도 사용할 수 있습니다.
When you get out of the Dharma hall, please return the prayer beads. Then other people can use them.

▶ ~한 지 ~이/가 되었어요. **It's been ~ since ~.**

서울에 도착한 지 1년이 되었습니다. It's been one year since I arrived in Seoul.

수행을 시작한 지 5년이 되었습니다. It's been five years since I started practice.

이 절의 주지가 된 지 3년 반이 되었습니다. It's been three and a half years since I became the abbot of this temple.

▶ 아마 ~ 때문일지도 모르겠군요. **It might be due to** 명사

아마 시차 때문인지도 모르겠군요. It might be due to the jetlag.

아마 날씨 때문인지도 모르겠군요. It might be due to the weather.

▶ 아마 ~ 하는 것이 나을 겁니다. **It would be better for you to** 부정사

아마 운동을 하는 게 나을 겁니다. It would be better for you to exercise.

아마 버스를 타는 게 나을 겁니다. It would be better for you to take a bus.

아마도 경전공부를 하는 게 나을 겁니다. It would be better for you to study Buddhist sutras.

아마 한 곳에 머무는 게 훨씬 나을 겁니다. It would be better for you to stay at one place.

▶ 듣고 보니~ 하는 것 같군요. **It sounds like ~.**

듣고 보니 그 사람이 많이 아픈 것 같군요. It sounds like he is very ill.

듣고 보니 그 절에 사람이 매우 많은 것 같군요. It sounds like the temple has so many people.

듣고 보니 수행하기가 쉬운 일은 아닌 것 같군요. It sounds like it's not easy to practice.

듣고 보니 해야 할 일이 많을 것 같군요. It sounds like there are a lot of things to be done.

▶ 알겠어요/그러죠. **I'll do that.**

Pair Work   Practice by substituting the underlined words with the proper words and phrases.

Sunim: What's the problem?

Martin: It's been five days since I arrived in India, but I've often had a stomachache.

Sunim: It might be due to the different water here. It would be better for you to drink boiled water.

Martin: I did, but I still have the problem.

Sunim: Then, it might be due to the spicy food here.

Martin: What can I do?

Sunim: Try eating rice porridge for a day or two and relax!

Martin: Thanks! I'll do that.

서산 대사의 게송

배고프면 밥을 먹고 곤하면 잠을 자네.

맑은 물 푸른 산을 내 멋대로 오가고

어촌과 주막거리도 내 집인 양 편하구나.

세월이 가나오나 내 알 바 아니건만

봄이 오니 예전처럼 풀잎 다시 푸르네.

– 《선가귀감(禪家龜鑑)》

Eating when hungry, sleeping when tired

Calling on clear waters and green mountains on a whim

I make myself at home either in the fishing villages

Or in the roads lined with taverns

I pay no attention to the coming and going of time

Yet spring is here, and the grass is green again as before.

- Master Seosan from the *Mirror for Seon Students*

1 절하는 법

(법당에서 절하는 스님을 보고)

잭슨: 스님 뭐하시는 거예요?

스님: 절합니다. 잭슨도 한번 해볼래요?

잭슨: 어떻게 하는 건가요?

스님: 먼저 선 채로 손을 모아 합장을 합니다. 그런 다음, 인사를 하면서 무릎을 굽히고 앉으세요. 그리고 오른손 왼손을 바닥에 내려요. 그 다음 머리를 조아려서 바닥에 닿게 하지요. 손바닥을 펴서 하늘을 보게 해서 귀까지 올린 뒤 다시 합장하고 일어나면 됩니다. 따라해 볼래요?

잭슨: 우와. 너무 어려워요.

Unit 1 **The Way of Prostration**

(Looking at the monk bowing in the Dharma hall)

Jackson: Sunim, what are you doing?

Sunim: I'm prostrating. Do you want to try too, Jackson?

Jackson: How should I do it?

Sunim: First, put your palms together while standing. And then, kneel on both your knees and bend your back over to prostrate and put both your hands on the floor. Then put your head down to the floor as well. Turn your palms up and raise your hands up under your ears and then put your palms together and stand up. Would you like to try?

Jackson: Wow... It's so difficult.

▶ 무엇을 하고 있나요? **What be + 주어 doing?**

그는 무엇을 하고 있나요? What is he doing?

스님들은 지금 무엇을 하고 있나요? What are the monks and nuns doing now?

아이들은 법당에서 무엇을 하고 있나요? What are the children doing in the Dharma hall?

▶ 지금 ～하고 있어요. **be ~ ing**

저는 아침 공양하고 있어요. I'm having breakfast.

저는 법당에서 염불하고 있어요. I'm chanting in the Dharma hall.

▶ 당신도 ～하고 싶은가요? **Do you want to ~, too?**

당신도 가고 싶습니까? Do you want to go, too?

당신도 수미산에 가고 싶습니까? Do you want to go to Mt. Sumeru, too?

당신도 하안거에 참여하고 싶습니까? Do you want to participate in the summer retreat, too?

▶ ～을 (내려)놓다. **put ~ down**

모자를 책상 위에 놓으세요. Please put your hat down on the table.

가방을 문쪽에 놓으세요. Please put your bag down near the door.

▶ ～을 돌려 위로 향하게 하다. **turn ~ up**

볼륨을 크게 높이세요. Turn the dial up for louder volume (Turn up the volume).

고개를 들어 별을 보세요. Turn you head up to see the stars.

▶ 손을 드세요. **raise your hand (up)**

아픈 사람은 손을 드세요. Please raise your hand (up) if you feel sick.

질문 있는 분은 손을 드십시오. Please raise your hand (up) if you have a question.

▶ ～을 하고 싶으십니까? **Would you like to ~?**

여행을 가고 싶습니까? Would you like to travel?

수련복을 사시겠습니까? Would you like to buy the temple uniform?

석굴암을 보러 가시겠습니까? Would you like to go to see the *Seokguram* grotto?

Pair Work Practice by substituting the underlined words with other proper words and phrases.

Jackson: Sunim, what are you doing?

Sunim: I'm weeding the garden. Do you want to help, Jackson?

Jackson: How should I do it?

Sunim: Do as I do.

(making lotus lanterns, cleaning Buddhist utencils, threading prayer beads)

2 목탁

(법당 밖에서)

잭슨: 지금 법당에서 울리는 소리가 뭐예요?

스님: 목탁소리 말이군요.

잭슨: 뭐에 쓰이는 거죠?

스님: 스님들이 의식을 행할 때 두드려서 소리를 내는 거랍니다.

잭슨: 소리가 아주 맑고 투명한 느낌이에요.

스님: 스님들이 의식을 할 때도 쓰이지만, 식사시간을 알릴 때에도 쓰인답니다.
목탁소리가 나면 식사하러 오세요.

잭슨: 목탁소리를 들으니 벌써 배가 고픈데요.

Unit 2 Moktak, the Wooden Handbell

(Outside of the Dharma hall)

Jackson: What's the sound from the Dharma hall?

Sunim: It's the sound of a wooden handbell. It's called "moktak" in Korean.

Jackson: What is it for?

Sunim: It is for Buddhist ceremonies. Monks and nuns hit it to make a sound during ceremonies.

Jackson: It sounds very clean and pure.

Sunim: Monks and nuns use it not only for Buddhist ceremonies but also for the announcement of meal times in temples. When you hear the wooden handbell (*moktak*) sound, please come for the meal.

Jackson: Listening to the sound of the wooden handbell(*moktak*), I feel like I'm already hungry.

▶ ~에서 들리는 저 소리가 무엇인가요? **What's the sound from ~?**

산에서 들리는 저 소리가 무엇인가요? What's the sound from the mountain?

요사채에서 들리는 저 소리는 무엇인가요? What's the sound from the living quarters?

▶ 그것은 ~을 위한 것입니다. **It is for ~.**

그것은 수행을 위한 것입니다. It is for the practice.

그것은 외국인의 템플스테이 홍보를 위한 것입니다. It is for the promotion of Templestays for non-Koreans (foreigners).

▶ 소리가 아주 ~ 합니다. **It sounds very ~.**

소리가 아주 흥쾌하군요. It sounds very exciting.

소리가 몹시 시끄럽군요. It sounds very noisy.

소리가 꽤 편안하군요. It sounds very comfortable.

▶ ~뿐만 아니라 ~도 **not only ~ but (also) ~**

그 책은 스님들뿐만 아니라 일반 신도들도 위해 있는 것이다. The book is not only for the monks and nuns but for lay Buddhists.

역사적으로 불교는 한국뿐만 아니라 다른 나라에도 전파가 되었다. Buddhism spread not only to Korea but also to other nations in history.

▶ ~ 소리를 들으니 ~ 기분이네요. **Listening to ~, I feel (like) ~.**

그 음악을 들으니 춤추고 싶네요. Listening to the music, I feel like dancing.

그 법문을 들으니 수행을 더 해야겠다는 생각이 듭니다. Listening to the Dharma talk, I feel like I should practice harder.

▶ 불교의식, 예불 **Buddhist ceremony**

▶ 목탁 **wooden handbell**

Pair Work Practice by substituting the underlined words with other proper words and phrases.

Jackson: What's the sound from the outside?

Sunim: It's the sound of a Buddhist bell. It's called *beomjong* in Korean.

Jackson: What is that for?

Sunim: It is sounded for all sentient beings suffering from the hell-like world.

Jackson: Listening to the Buddhist bell sound, I feel very calm.

3 염주

애나: 스님 손에 있는 것이 무엇인가요?

스님: 이것은 염주라고 합니다.

애나: 염주? 무엇을 하는 것이죠?

스님: 이렇게 돌리면서 기도를 하거나 절을 할 때 사용합니다.

애나: 그럼, 염주 알은 몇 개나 되나요?

스님: 이것처럼 긴 것은 108개이고요,
　　　손목에 하는 것은 숫자에 제한이 없습니다.

애나: 둘 다 염주라고 부르나요?

스님: 네, 다만 손목에 하는 짧은 염주는 합장주라고 부릅니다.

Unit 3 Prayer Beads

Anna: Sunim, What are you holding in your hands?

Sunim: They are prayer beads called "yeomju" in Korean.

Anna: "Yeomju"? What do you do with that?

Sunim: You turn each bead as you pray or prostrate.

Anna: Then how many beads are in it?

Sunim: This long one has 108 beads but a small chain of prayer beads for the wrist does not have any fixed number of beads.

Anna: Do you call them both "yeomju"?

Sunim: Yes, you could. But generally the short wrist prayer beads are called a "hapjangju".

▶ 그것을 무엇에 씁니까? **What do you do with ~?**

▶ 이것은 ~라고 부릅니다. **This is called ~**

이 옷은 가사라고 부릅니다. These are ceremonial robes called kasaya.

이 경전은 《화엄경》이라고 합니다. This sutra is called *the Avatamsaka Sutra.*

이 부처님상은 미륵부처님이라고 합니다. This statue of the Buddha is called the Maitreya Buddha, or the Future Buddha.

▶ 몇 개/명이 ~ 안에 있습니까? **How many ~ are in it?**

몇 분의 스님이 그곳에 계십니까? How many monks are in the temple?

▶ 아직 ~가 정해지지 않았다. **~ hasn't been fixed yet.**

그는 아직 회의시간을 정하지 않았다. He hasn't fixed the time of our meeting.

재를 올릴 날짜는 아직 정해지지 않았다. No date has yet been fixed for the ceremony.

교통사고로 들어온 그 차는 아직 고쳐지지 않았다. The car from the accident hasn't been fixed yet.

Sunim, What are you holding in your hands?

They are prayer beads called "yeomju" in Korean.

Pair Work Practice by substituting the underlined words with other proper words and phrases.

Anna: Sunim, What are you holding in your hands?

Sunim: It is a wind chime. It's called "punggyeong" in Korean.

Anna: "Punggyeong"? What do you do with that?

Sunim: It will be hung on the eaves of the temple roof.

Anna: Oh, I see. It makes a beautiful sound when the wind blows.

4 합장

스님: 불교에서는 서로 인사를 할 때 합장을 합니다.

마틴: 어떻게 하는 거죠?

스님: 따라해보세요.

먼저 가슴 앞에서 손바닥과 손바닥이 마주보도록 양손을 모아보세요.

마틴: 이렇게요?

스님: 네, 아주 자세가 좋은데요.

마틴: 합장을 하는 의미가 있나요?

스님: 그럼요. 오른손은 부처님 마음, 왼손은 내 마음을 나타낸다고 하지요.

부처님과 내가 하나가 된다는 의미가 있어요.

마틴: 아, 중요한 의미가 담겨 있군요.

Unit 4 Holding Palms Together

Sunim: When Buddhists greet, they put their palms together and greet each other. It's called "hapjang" in Korean.

Martin: How do they do it?

Sunim: Follow me, please. First put your palms together at your chest.

Martin: Like this?

Sunim: Right. You're doing very well.

Martin: Is there any meaning in holding palms together?

Sunim: Yes. The right hand means the Buddha's mind; the left hand means my mind.

That way both the Buddha and myself become one mind.

Martin: I see. It has a very significant meaning.

▶ ~ 할 때, ~ 한다.

그가 나를 처음 보았을 때, 그는 내게 합장하여 인사하였다. When he looked at me at first, he greeted me by holding his palms together.

그가 법당 안에 들어갔을 때, 그는 향냄새를 맡았다. When he entered the Dharma hall, he smelled the incense.

신도님들이 향천사를 갈 때, 스님들을 위해 승복을 준비하여 갔다. When the Buddhists went to Hyangcheon-sa Temple, they prepared monastic robes for the monks.

▶ 방법과 수단을 나타내는 how

그곳에 어떻게 가야 합니까? How do you get there?

기차역에 어떻게 갑니까? How do I get to the train station?

이것을 어떻게 가져가지요? How do I take this?

참선은 어떻게 합니까? How do I do meditation?

가사는 어떻게 입습니까? How do I wear *kasaya*?

▶ 그것은 아주 중요한 의미가 있군요. **It has a very significant meaning.**

▶ 가슴에 **at one's chest**

Is there any
meaning in holding
palms together?

Pair Work   Free Response

1. How do you do hapjang?
2. When you greet someone in the temple, do you usually shake hands?
3. How do you get to the train station from the temple?
4. How do you do meditation?
5. How do you sit in the lotus position?

5 가사

마틴: 스님, 지금 입고 계신 옷은 매우 멋진데요?

스님: 그런가요? 이 옷은 가사라고 합니다.

마틴: 평소에는 이 옷을 안 입고 있었던 것 같은데요.

스님: 네, 이 옷은 불교의식을 행할 때만 입습니다.

마틴: 스님들의 가사는 다 같은 모양인가요?

스님: 언뜻 보기에는 모두 같아 보이지만, 자세히 보면 다 다릅니다.

마틴: 왜 다르죠?

스님: 출가한 지 오래되신 분일수록 더 조각이 많답니다.

마틴: 아, 그렇군요.

Unit 5 Ceremonial Robes

Martin: Sunim, the clothes you're wearing now are very cool!

Sunim: Do you think so? These clothes are ceremonial robes called "kasaya".

Martin: I don't think you wear them ordinarily.

Sunim: You are right. Monks and nuns wear these clothes only when they do a Buddhist ceremony.

Martin: Do monks and nuns all wear the same looking clothes?

Sunim: They all look the same at a glance, but they are all different if you look at them carefully.

Martin: Why are they all different?

Sunim: The longer one lives as a monk or nun, the more pieces are added.

Martin: Oh, I see.

Words & Phrases

▶ '착용하다'의 **wear**

당신이 끼고 있는 장갑이 정말 멋집니다! The gloves you're wearing are very cool!

당신이 쓰고 있는 모자가 정말 멋집니다! The hat you're wearing is very cool!

당신이 끼고 있는 선글라스가 정말 멋집니다! The sunglasses you're wearing are very cool!

▶ 제 생각으로 평소에는 ~하지 않는 것 같습니다. **I don't think--- ordinarily**

제 생각에는 평소에 그것을 사용하지 않는 것 같습니다. I don't think you use it ordinarily.

제 생각에는 평소에 그곳에 가지 않는 것 같습니다. I don't think you go there ordinarily.

제 생각에는 평소에 그것을 먹지 않는 것 같습니다. I don't think you eat it ordinarily.

▶ 얼핏 보면 그들은 모두 ~ 해 보인다. **They all look ~ at a glance.**

얼핏 보면 그들은 모두 바빠 보입니다. They all look busy at a glance.

얼핏 보면 그들은 모두 행복해 보입니다. They all look happy at a glance.

얼핏 보면 그들은 모두 화나 보입니다. They all look upset at a glance.

▶ 더 오래 ~할수록, 더 ~ 해진다. **The longer ~, the more ~.**

컴퓨터를 더 오래 사용할수록, 더 잘 알 수 있습니다. The longer you use a computer, the more you understand it.

더 오래 수행할수록, 더 많이 배운다. The longer you practice, the more you learn.

더 오랫동안 일할수록, 돈을 더 많이 번다. The longer you work, the more you earn.

Pair Work Practice by substituting the underlined words with other proper words and phrases.

Sunim: Martin, the gloves you're wearing are nice!

Martin: Thank you, Sunim.

Sunim: I don't think you wear them ordinarily.

Martin: You are right. I wear them only when I work with tools.

53

6 반배

(산행 후 사찰에 도착)

마틴: 드디어 도착했다. 산행하는 데 3시간이나 걸렸네.

(스님이 사찰 입구에서 반배를 한다.)

마틴: (스님을 바라보며) 스님, 입구에서도 인사를 해야 하나요?

스님: 외출했다가 돌아온 후에도 '잘 다녀왔습니다.' 하고 절 입구에서 법당을 향해 반배를 드립니다.

마틴: 반배는 고개만 숙이면 되나요?

스님: 아뇨. 반배는 합장을 한 채로 머리를 숙여 예를 갖추는 것입니다.

마틴: 절 입구에서만 하면 되나요?

스님: 법당에 들어갈 때나 나올 때, 도량에서 스님을 만났을 때, 그리고 탑 앞에서도 합니다.

Unit 6 Half Bow

(Arriving at the temple after mountain climbing)

Martin: Wow... finally we're here. It took 3 hours of climbing to get here.

(The monk is offering a half bow in front of the temple gate)

Martin: (Watching monk's bowing) Sunim, should I bow at the gate as well?

Sunim: When you come back from going out, you should say "I'm home" by offering a half bow at the gate towards the Dharma hall.

Martin: For a half bow, should I bend my neck only?

Sunim: No, you should put your palms together and bend your back over politely.

Martin: Should I do it only at the entrance gate of the temple?

 Sunim: When you get in and out of the Dharma hall, when you meet monks and nuns around temples, and also in front of pagodas.

Words & Phrases

▶ ~ 하는 데 ~가 걸렸다. **It took ~ to 부정사 (to + 동사 원형)**.

산책하는 데 2시간이 걸렸어요. It took 2 hours to take a walk.

수행하는 데 5년이 걸렸어요. It took 5 years to practice.

이사하는 데 이틀이 걸렸어요. It took two days to move.

▶ 저도 ~ 해야 하나요? **Should I ~ as well?**

저도 가야 하나요? Should I go as well?

저도 그를 따라가야 하나요? Should I follow him as well?

저도 그 회의에 참석해야 하나요? Should I attend the conference as well?

For a half bow, should I bend my neck only?

You should put your palms together and bend your back over politely.

Pair Work Free Respons

1. How long does it take to do the early morning ceremony?
2. Does it take 30 minutes to finish the dinner?
3. How long does it take to cook the rice?
4. How long does it take from the temple to the nearby village on foot?
5. How long does it take to climb to the top of the mountain?

Chapter **4** **Temple Living** 사찰 생활

1 발우공양

스님: 오늘 점심은 발우공양으로 하겠습니다.

마틴: 발우공양이 무엇인가요?

스님: 발우공양은 스님들의 전통 식사법입니다.

마틴: 어떻게 하죠?

스님: 자, 나를 보면서 따라 하세요.

Unit 1 Baru Gongyang, Formal Monastic Meal

Sunim: Today we will have lunch in the *baru gongyang* style.

Martin: What's *baru gongyang*?

Sunim: *Baru gongyang* is a traditional method of eating a meal for Buddhist monks and nuns.

Martin: How do I do it?

Sunim: Here, please watch me and do as I do.

▶ 발우공양 **formal monastic meal, traditional momastic meal, traditional-style meal for Buddhist monks and nuns**

오늘 아침은 발우공양으로 하겠습니다. Today we will have breakfast in the traditional monastic style (formal monatic style, *baru gongyang* style).

▶ 오늘 점심은 ~로 하겠습니다. **We will have ~ for lunch today.**

오늘 점심은 비빔밥이 되겠습니다. We will have *bibimbap* for lunch today.

내일 점심은 피자가 되겠습니다. We will have pizza for lunch tomorrow.

※ 구체적으로 어떤 음식을 먹는 것에 대해 강조하고 싶을 땐 'eat'을 쓴다.

ex) 김치를 먹을 거예요. I will eat *kimchi*.

된장찌개가 먹고 싶어요. I'd like to eat *doenjang jjigae*.

▶ 무엇인가요? **What is/ are ~?**

아미타불이란 무엇인가요? What is Amitabha Buddha?

삼보란 무엇인가요? What are the Three Jewels?

삼보사찰이란 무엇인가요? What are the Three Jewel Temples?

▶ (그것을) 어떻게 합니까?

제가 그것을 어떻게 하죠? How do I do it?

그는 그것을 어떻게 합니까? How does he do it?

찬불가를 어떻게 따라 부릅니까? How do I follow the Buddhist hymn?

▶ (저를) 따라 하세요. **Please watch me and do as I do. / Please follow me as I do.**

▶ (저를) 보세요/보십시오. **Watch (me), please.**

▶ 배추 **Chinese cabbage**

▶ 한국 전통 발효음식 **a traditional fermented Korean dish**

▶ 갖은 양념 **various seasonings**

Pair Work Practice by substituting the underlined words.

Martin: What's *kimchi*?
Sunim: *Kimchi* is a traditional fermented Korean dish made with Chinese cabbage and various seasonings.
Martin: How do I eat it?
Sunim: Here, please watch me and do as I do.

2 공양 게송

스님: 공양을 하기 전에는 '오관게' 라고 하는 게송을 외웁니다.

마틴: 기독교인들이 밥 먹기 전에 신께 기도하는 것과 같은 것인가요?

스님: 네, 그와 유사합니다. 하지만 불교에서는 신뿐만 아니라, 모두에게 감사하죠.

마틴: 그 내용을 알려주세요.

스님: 자, 그럼 따라 하세요. 이 음식이 어디서 왔는가?

마틴: 이 음식이 어디서 왔는가?

　　　내 덕행으로 받기가 부끄럽네.

　　　어떤 마음으로 내가 이 음식을 받아야 하는가.

　　　내 몸의 수행에 영양분을 주는 약으로 알아 이 음식을 받네.

　　　나는 다른 이들을 돕기 위해 이 음식을 어떻게 사용해야 하는가.

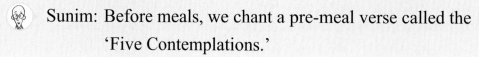

Unit 2 Pre-Meal Chant

Sunim: Before meals, we chant a pre-meal verse called the 'Five Contemplations.'

Martin: Is it similar to Christians praying to God before they eat?

Sunim: It is similar, but in Buddhism, we thank all beings as well as God.

Martin: Please explain the content of the meal verse.

Sunim: Sure! Here, please repeat after me. Where does all this food come from?...

Martin: Where does all this food come from?

I'm not worthy to receive it of my own virtue and practice.

In what spirit should I accept this food?

I accept this food as medicine to sustain my body for practice.

How can I use this food to help others?

Words & Phrases

▶ 공양 게송 **Pre-meal Chant**

▶ '오관게' **the Five Contemplations**

▶ '게송을 외다.' **chant a verse/chant verses**

▶ '기독교인(들)' **Christian(s)**

▶ A는 B와 비슷한가요? **Is A similar to B?**

송광사와 해인사는 비슷한 점이 있나요? Is Songgwang-sa Temple similar to Haein-sa Temple?

빈대떡과 전(지짐)은 비슷한 건가요? Is *Bindaetteok* similar to vegetable pancake?

당신의 여행일정과 현공 스님의 일정은 비슷한가요? Is your traveling plan similar to Hyeongong sunim's plan?

▶ 네, 유사합니다. **Yes, it's similar.**

※ 아주 유사합니다. (의견일치를 분명히 하고자 할 때) Absolutely!!

▶ ～를 알려주세요. **Please explain** [간접목적어/명사/대명사] + [명사구/명사절].

그 사람에게 어떻게 절하는지 알려주세요. Please explain to him how to prostrate.

그 법문 후 어디로 가야하는지 좀 가르쳐주세요. Please explain to me where to go after the Dharma talk.

왜 스님이 되셨는지 저희들에게 좀 말씀해주세요. Please explain to us why you've become a monk.

▶ 따라 하세요. (행동을 따라 하라는 경우에) **(Please) do as I do.**

따라 하세요. (말을 따라 하라는 경우에) (Please) repeat after me.

～가 어디서 왔는가? Where does 명사/대명사 come from? 과거부터 현재까지 앞으로도 계속해서 일어나는 일 등은 '현재의 불변'으로 현재시제를 쓴다.

Cf. Where did the parcel come from? (그 소포가 어디서 왔습니까?)

It was delivered from Seoul yesterday. (그것은 어제 서울에서 배달된 것입니다).

▶ 불자(들) **Buddhists**

▶ 힌두교도(들) **Hindu(s)**

▶ 나는 ～ 할 자격이 없다. **I'm not worthy to** 동사 원형 **/ I'm not worthy of** 명사(구)

나는 (아직) 오계를 받을 자격이 없습니다. I'm not worthy to receive the five precepts.

나는 그 상을 받을 자격이 없습니다. I'm not worthy of the prize.

▶ **as ~**   ～으로

나는 그 음식을 간식으로 먹었어요. I had the food as a snack.

나는 그 스님을 부모님처럼 대해 드렸어요. I treated the Sunim as my parent.

Pair Work   Practice by substituting the underlined words with other proper words.

Sunim: Buddhists pray to the Buddha.

Martin: Is it similar to Hindus praying to Krishna?

Sunim: Yes it is.

Martin: Where did the Buddha come from?

Sunim: The Buddha came from India.

無窮山下泉　普供山中侶

各持一瓢來　總得全月去

다함이 없는 산하의 샘물을

널리 산중의 벗(도반)들에게 공양하노니

각기 표주박 하나씩을 가지고 와서

모두 온달(보름달)을 건져가소서.

A mountain spring wells forth clear water
endlessly
I offer this water to the friends of mountains
Please bring a bottle gourd with you
And take a full moon out of the spring.

3 시간 지키기

잭슨: 저녁은 몇 시에 먹나요?

스님: 5시 30분에 먹습니다.

잭슨: 그럼, 예불시간은 언제죠?

스님: 예불은 6시 45분부터 시작합니다.

잭슨: 그럼, 그때까지 뭘 하면 되지요?

스님: 저녁공양 하고, 자기 방 정돈을 하세요. 산책을 하셔도 좋습니다.

잭슨: 멀리까지 가도 됩니까?

스님: 산문 밖을 벗어나면 안 되고, 예불시간은 꼭 지키셔야 합니다.

Unit 3 Being on Time

Jackson: What time is dinner?

Sunim: We eat at 5: 30 pm.

Jackson: Then what time is the evening Buddhist ceremony?

Sunim: It begins at 6: 45 pm.

Jackson: Well, what can I do until then?

Sunim: After the evening meal, tidy up your room. You could also go for a walk.

Jackson: May I go far?

Sunim: Do not go beyond the temple gate, and you should be on time for the Buddhist ceremony.

▶ ~은 몇 시예요? **What time is ~?**

1교시는 몇 시예요? What time is the first period class?

법회는 몇 시예요? What time is the Dharma gathering?

※ 아침 / 점심 / 저녁을 먹다. have (eat) breakfast / lunch / dinner

▶ 예불 **(the) Buddhist ceremony**

▶ 저녁예불 **evening (Buddhist) ceremony**

▶ ~를 정돈하세요. **tidy up ~** / ※ **clean up** (완전히 청소하라는 의미)

법당을 정돈하세요. Would (Could) you tidy up the Dharma hall? (공손한 부탁형)

※ 법당 정돈 좀 합시다! (제안형) Let's tidy up the Dharma hall.

법당 청소하세요! (명령형) Tidy up the Dharma hall!

교실을 청소하세요. Would you clean up the classroom?

▶ ~시부터 시작하다. **starts at ~**

저녁 예불은 6시에 시작합니다. Evening (Buddhist) ceremony starts at 6 pm.

참선은 새벽 5시에 시작합니다. Seon meditation starts at 5 am.

Pair Work Practice by substituting the underlined words with other proper words.

Jackson: What time is breakfast?

Sunim: Breakfast begins at 5:00 am.

Jackson: What can I do until then?

Sunim: Please, tidy up the temple, and make sure you don't go out too far if you want to go for a walk.

Jackson: Then what time is lunch?

Sunim: Lunch begins at 11:00 am.

Jackson: Thanks.

4 사찰에서 금해야 할 것

잭슨: (혼잣말로) 너무 덥고 갈증 나는데, 시원한 맥주 한 잔 마시면 좋겠다.

스님: 뭐라고요?

잭슨: 아니요, 너무 더워서 맥주 한 잔하고 싶어서요. 사찰에서는 안 되겠지요?

스님: 네, 사찰에서는 술을 마셔서도 안 되고, 담배를 피워서도 안 됩니다.

잭슨: 친구들과 이야기하는 것은 괜찮지요?

스님: 큰 소리로 떠드는 건 안 되지만, 목소리를 낮추어서 조용히 말하면 됩니다.

잭슨: 사찰에서는 금해야 할 것들이 많군요.

Unit 4 Things not to Do in Temples

Jackson: (Speaking to himself) It's so hot and I'm thirsty. I'd love to have just one cold beer.

Sunim: Excuse me?

Jackson: Oh, it's very hot, so I said I wanted a beer. But that's not allowed in the temple, right?

Sunim: Yes, you must not drink alcohol or smoke inside the temple.

Jackson: Is it OK to talk with my friends?

Sunim: Yes, but do not talk loudly. Speak in a hushed tone.

Jackson: I see there are many things to refrain from in the temple.

▶ 목이 마르다. / 갈증이 나다. **I'm thirsty.**

   ~을 하고 싶다. **I want to 부정사 (to + 동사 원형).**

   차를 마시고 싶습니다. I want to drink some tea.

   산책을 가고 싶습니다. I want to go for a walk.

▶ (술) 마시다. **drink (alcohol)**

   그는 술을 자주 마십니다. He drinks very often.

   그는 술을 며칠 전에 끊었습니다. He stopped drinking a few days ago.

▶ 담배를 피우다. **smoke** / 담배를 피우는 행위 **smoking** (동명사)

   그는 담배를 하루에 한번 피웁니다. He smokes (a cigarette) once a day.

   그는 담배를 1년 전에 끊었습니다. He quit smoking a year ago.

▶ 큰(작은) 소리로 말하다. **talk loudly (quietly)**

   스님은 절에서 조용히 말합니다. Sunim talks quietly in temples.

   그 남자는 절에서 너무 시끄럽게 말합니다. He talks too loudly in temples.

▶ 조용한 목소리 **hushed tone**

▶ ~이군요. **I see ~**

▶ ~하는 것을 삼가다. **refrain from ~**

   그는 담배를 끊으려고 무척 노력하고 있어요. He's trying hard to refrain from smoking.

Pair **W**ork Practice by substituting the underlined words with other words and phrases.

   Jackson: It's very hot and I'm tired. I want to drink wine.

   Sunim: Drinking wine is not allowed in the temple.

   Jackson: Is it OK to listen to music?

   Sunim: Yes, but you must not do it loudly. Listen quietly.

   Jackson: OK. Thanks!

5 삭발

애나: 머리카락이 더 짧아지셨네요.

스님: 네, 삭발을 했습니다.

애나: 스님들은 혼자서 머리를 깎으시나요?

스님: 혼자 깎기도 하고 서로 깎아주기도 합니다.

애나: 그런데 스님들은 머리를 왜 깎는 것이죠?

스님: 머리카락이 길면 수행에 방해되기 때문이랍니다.

Unit 5 Head-Shaving

Anna: I see your hair has gotten shorter again.

Sunim: Yes, I shaved my head.

Anna: Do monks shave their own heads?

Sunim: Sometimes we do it alone, and sometimes we shave each other's.

Anna: But why do monks shave their heads?

Sunim: Because long hair can disturb Buddhist practice.

▶ 〜이군요. **I see ~**

살이 좀 빠지신 거 같군요. I see you've lost some weight.

건강이 많이 좋아지신 거 같군요. I see you've become much healthier.

▶ 짧아졌다. **gotten shorter** / 길어졌다. **gotten longer**

낮이 짧아졌어요. The day has gotten shorter.

밤이 길어지고 있어요. The night is getting longer.

▶ 면도하다(삭발하다.) **shave (one's head)**

그는 어제 면도를 하였다. He shaved his beard yesterday.

그 스님은 어제 삭발하였다. The Sunim shaved his head yesterday.

▶ 방해가 되다, 방해하다. **disturb**

제 수행을 방해하지 마십시오. Don't disturb my practice.

그 아기의 울음이 버스 안의 모든 승객들을 방해했다. The baby's crying disturbed the passengers in the bus.

▶ 혼자 **alone**

나는 혼자 살 수 없어요. I can't live alone.

그는 동생이 죽고 난 후 혼자가 되어 버렸다. He became alone after his brother died.

▶ 가끔 **sometimes**

참선 중 그는 조금씩 쉬는 시간을 가진다. During meditation, sometimes he takes a break.

Pair Work   Practice by substituting the underlined words with other proper words.

Anna: I see your hair has gotten longer.

Sunim: Yes. I have to shave again.

Anna: Will you shave alone?

Sunim: Yes, I will shave alone.

Anna: Do you always shave alone?

Sunim: Well, sometimes I shave alone.

6 단청과 탱화

애나: 한국 절은 화려해요.

스님: 왜 그렇게 생각하죠?

애나: 형형색색으로 꾸며져 있잖아요.

스님: 아, 단청 말이군요.

애나: 저 법당 안에 있는 그림도 그렇고요.
　　　저 그림은 뭐라고 하죠?

스님: 저건 탱화라고 합니다.
　　　불보살님의 모습을 그린 것이죠.

애나: 아, 이런 것들 다 배우려면 시간이 오래 걸리겠군요.

Unit 6 Dancheong and Buddhist Painting

Anna:　Korean temples are colorful.

Sunim:　Why do you think so?

Anna:　They are painted very brightly.

Sunim:　Oh, you're talking about *dancheong*, multi-colored temple paintwork.

Anna:　The painting inside the Dharma hall over there is also colorful. What do you call that picture?

Sunim:　That is called *taenghwa*, Buddhist paintings of Buddhas and Bodhisattvas.

Anna:　Gosh! It's going to take a long time to learn all these things.

▶ 화려한(색깔을 의미), 형형색색의 **colorful**

The Lotus Lantern Festival is rather colorful. 연등축제는 몹시 화려합니다.

▶ 환하게 **brightly**

그녀는 환하게 웃는다. She smiles brightly.

관세음보살님이 화사하게 미소 짓고 계시는 듯하다. I feel like Avalokitesvara Bodhisattva smiles brightly.

▶ 법당 **Dharma hall**

▶ 대웅전 **Main Buddha Hall**

▶ 오래 걸리다. **take a long time**

그 예불이 끝나려면 시간이 오래 걸릴 거에요. It will take a long time to finish the (Buddhist) ceremony.

그곳에 가려면 시간이 꽤 걸릴 거에요. It will take a long time to get there.

▶ 부르다. **call**

주지스님이 지금 부르십니다. The Abbot of the temple is calling you.

▶ ~라고 부르다. **is called ~**

그것은 목탁이라고 합니다. It is called a *moktak*, wooden handbell.

거기는 대웅전이라고 부릅니다. It is called the Main Buddha Hall.

▶ ~하는 데 얼마나 걸려요? **How long does it take to** 부정사(**to** + 동사 원형)

그 독송을 끝내려면 얼마나 걸리죠? How long does it take to finish chanting?

그것을 요리하는 데 얼마나 걸려요? How long does it take to cook?

108배를 하는 데 시간이 얼마 걸립니까? How long does it take to prostrate 108 times?

Pair Work Practice by substituting the underlined words with other proper words and phrases.

Anna: The Main Buddha Hall is so colorful.

Sunim: All Korean temples are painted brightly.

Anna: How long does it take to paint the temple?

Sunim: Painting the temple takes a long time. Sometimes 20 years.

Anna: Gosh! That's a long time!

Chapter 5 Buddhist Practice 수행

1 출가

마틴: 스님, 한국불교 스님들은 결혼을 하나요?

스님: 결혼을 허용하는 종단도 있지만, 조계종 스님들은 결혼을 하지 않습니다.

마틴: 그럼 조계종 스님들은 모두가 독신인가요?

스님: 그렇죠.

마틴: 이혼을 한 경우는요?

스님: 이혼을 했거나 사별한 경우에는 출가하여 스님이 될 수 있습니다.

Unit 1 Renouncing the Secular Life

Martin: Sunim, do monks in Korea get married?

Sunim: Some Buddhist orders allow marriage, but monks of the Jogye Order do not get married.

Martin: Then all the monks of the Jogye Order are single?

Sunim: That's correct.

Martin: What about divorced people?

Sunim: Divorced people or people whose spouses have died can renounce the secular life and become monastics.

▶ 결혼을 하다. **get married** (결혼을 한 행위에 중점)

그는 3년 전에 결혼했습니다. He got married 3 years ago.

▶ 결혼을 하다. **be married** (결혼을 한 상태에 중점)

Are you married? 결혼하셨습니까?

Yes, I'm married. 네. (저는 유부남/유부녀입니다.)

대부분의 스님들은 모두 결혼을 하지 않았습니다.

Most monks and nuns are not married.

▶ 독신(이다.) **(be) single**

그들은 거의가 독신이다. They are mostly single.

그녀는 독신입니다. She is single.

▶ 그렇죠. **That's correct. / You're right.**

▶ 이혼하다. **divorce**

많은 이혼자들이 지금 그 절에서 수행을 하고 있습니다. A number of divorced people are doing practice at the temple for the moment.

▶ 배우자 **spouse**

제 배우자는 지금 어디 있죠? Where is my spouse?

그녀의 배우자는 매우 조용한 사람이다. Her spouse is a very quiet man.

▶ 출가하다(세속을 버리다.) **renounce the secular life**

▶ 세속 생활 **secular life**

▶ 수도승 생활 **monastic life**

Pair Work Practice by substituting the underlined words with other proper words and phrases.

Sunim: Are you married?

Martin: Yes, I am. Are you married, Sunim?

Sunim: No, I am not. I renounced the secular life.

Martin: I want to renounce the secular life, too.

Sunim: Divorced people can renounce the secular life.

Martin: I am not divorced. So I cannot become a monk?

Sunim: That's correct.

2 승가교육

마틴: 스님들은 무슨 공부를 하나요?

스님: 당연히 불교 공부, 마음공부를 합니다.

마틴: 구체적으로 말씀해주세요.

스님: 불교에서 말하는 공부란 부처님의 가르침뿐만 아니라,
　　　참선, 독경, 염불 등 일상수행에 관한 모든 것을 공부라고 하지요.

마틴: 전통적인 것만 공부하나요?

스님: 아니요. 요즘엔 외국어, 컴퓨터 등 스님들의 공부가 더 많아졌답니다.

Unit 2 Monastic Training

Martin: What do monks study?

Sunim: Obviously they study Buddhism and cultivate their
minds.

Martin: Could you be more specific?

Sunim: 'Study' in Buddhism refers to studying the Buddha's
teachings as well as performing Seon meditation,
recitation of scriptures, and chanting.

Martin: Do monks only study traditional subjects?

Sunim: No. Nowadays the subjects monks must study have
increased, including foreign languages, computers, and
other things.

▶ 더 자세히 **be more specific**

당신이 하고 있는 일에 대해 좀더 구체적으로 말해주십시오. Please be more specific about what you are doing.

그는 사찰 내에서의 예의범절에 대해 더 자세히 가르친다. He is more specific about his instructions regarding the temple etiquette.

▶ 언급하다, 의미하다. **refer to**

대승불교는 동아시아에서 주로 수행되는 불교라 할 수 있다. *Mahayana* refers to Buddhism practiced in East Asia.

그는 템플스테이 오리엔테이션에서 절에서의 규칙을 언급하였다. He referred to the temple rules during the Templestay orientation.

▶ ~만, 단지 **only**

▶ 요즘 **nowadays**

▶ 과목 **subject**

수학은 제가 좋아하는 과목이 아닙니다. Math is not my favorite subject.

고등학교 때 무슨 과목을 좋아했습니까? What was your favorite subject in high school?

▶ 독경 **recitation of scriptures**

▶ 염불 **chanting**

Pair Work Practice by substituting the underlined words with other proper words and phrases.

Sunim: What subjects did you study in school, Martin?
Martin: I studied world history and English.
Sunim: Nowadays monks study English, too.
Martin: I would like to study chanting.
Sunim: Good. Watch me and do as I do.

3 좌선하는 법

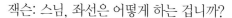

잭슨: 스님, 좌선은 어떻게 하는 겁니까?

스님: 좌선은 먼저 바르게 앉는 것에서 시작됩니다.

잭슨: 어떻게 앉아야 좌선의 바른 자세죠?

스님: 스님들은 좌선을 하기 위해 주로 반가부좌를 합니다. 반가부좌란 왼쪽 다리를
오른쪽 다리 위에 포개서 올려놓거나 오른쪽 다리를 왼쪽 다리 위에 포개 올려
놓는 것을 말합니다.

잭슨: 손은 어떻게 하죠?

스님: 손은 오른손이 왼손을 감싸도록 해서 둥글게 모양을 만든 다음, 단전 앞에
둡니다. 그리고 시선은 자연스럽게 앞쪽 바닥을 바라봅니다.

잭슨: 잘 안 돼요.

스님: 걱정 마세요. 자꾸 하다 보면 곧 익숙해실 겁니다.

Unit 3 How to Do Sitting Meditation

Jackson: Sunim, how can I do sitting meditation?

Sunim: Sitting meditation begins by sitting with a correct
posture.

Jackson: What is the correct posture for sitting meditation?

Sunim: When monks perform sitting meditation, they usually
sit in a half-lotus position. Half-lotus position means
that you cross your left leg over your right, or the right
leg over the left while seated.

Jackson: What about the hands?

Sunim: Your right hand should cover your left and your hands
should be gathered below your navel, forming a circle

with your arms. You should gaze comfortably at the floor in front of you.

 Jackson: It's difficult.

 Sunim:　Don't worry. If you keep doing it, you'll get used to it.

Words & Phrases

▶ **좌선 sitting meditation**

두 시간 동안 좌선합시다. Let's sit for 2 hours to meditate.

좌선과 걷기명상은 다릅니다. Sitting meditation is different from walking meditation.

▶ **자세 posture**

그의 자세는 그리 올바르지 않군요. His posture is not so correct.

당신의 좌선 자세는 아주 좋아요! Your sitting posture is awesome!

▶ **다리를 꼬다. cross (your) legs**

그녀는 의자에 앉을 때마다 다리를 꼬고 앉는다. Whenever she sits on a chair, she always crosses her legs.

▶ **반가부좌 half lotus position**

▶ **가부좌 full lotus position**

▶ **바라보다, 쳐다보다. gaze(at, up)**

좌선 시 다른 수행자들을 쳐다보려 하면 안 됩니다. Don't try to gaze at other practitioners when you sit.

해돋이를 바라보았을 때 나는 마치 천국에 온 것 같았다. As I gazed up at the sunrise, I felt like I was in heaven.

▶ **자연스럽게, 편안하게 comfortably**

▶ **걱정 마세요. Don't worry.**

당신이 한 실수에 대해 너무 걱정하지 마세요. Don't worry too much about your mistake.

집에 어떻게 갈지 너무 걱정마세요. 제가 차로 바래다 줄께요. Don't worry about how to get back home. I'll give you a lift.

※ 걱정을 너무 많이 하면, 해답을 찾을 수가 없답니다. If you worry too much, you can't see the answer.

▶ ~에 익숙해지다. **get used to ~** 명사형

자세에 대해 너무 걱정하지 마세요. 시간이 지나면서 다 익숙해질 겁니다.

Don't worry about your posture. You'll get used to it as time goes by.

나는 절에서 사는 게 조금씩 익숙해집니다. I'm getting used to living in the temple.

▶ 등을 (꼿꼿하게) 세우다.

좌선 수행을 할 때 등을 굽히지 않도록 조심하세요. When you practice sitting meditation make sure to keep your back straight.

Pair Work Practice by substituting the underlined words with other proper words and phrases.

Jackson: How can I sit with correct posture?

Sunim: Sit with your back straight.

Jackson: It's difficult.

Sunim: Don't worry. You will get used to it.

Jackson: Is my posture correct?

Sunim: Yes, it is.

성 안내는 그 얼굴이 참다운 공양구요,

부드러운 말 한마디 미묘한 향이로다.

깨끗해 티가 없는 진실한 그 마음이

언제나 한결같은 부처님 마음일세.

A face without any anger is a genuine offering
vessel,
A word of peacefulness is a subtle fragrance.
A clear, truthful mind without any speck of dust
Is the mind of Buddha that knows no fluctuation.

4 경전독송

(스님이 경전을 독송하고 있다.)

잭슨: 스님~

스님: (잭슨을 바라보며) 네~ 왔어요?

잭슨: 방해가 되지 않았나요?

스님: 아니에요. 괜찮습니다.

잭슨: 그 책은 뭔가요?

스님: 부처님 말씀이 담겨 있는 경전입니다. 《금강경》이라는 경전이에요.

잭슨: 저도 읽어보고 싶어요.

Unit 4 Reciting Buddhist Sutras

(The monk is reciting sutras.)

Jackson: Sunim!

Sunim: (looking at Jackson) Hi, Jackson!

Jackson: Am I bothering you?

Sunim: No, you're not. It's OK.

Jackson: What is that book?

Sunim: This is a sutra. It contains the Buddha's teachings.
         This particular sutra is called *the Diamond Sutra*.

Jackson: I would like to read it, too.

▶ 독송하다. **recite**

그는 자기 친구들 앞에서 절대로 자신의 시를 낭송하지 않는다.

He never recites his poems in front of his friends.

주지스님이 경을 읽을 때는 목소리가 몹시 깊고 맑으시다. When the abbot recites sutras, his voice becomes so deep and clear.

▶ 경전 **sutra**

아직까지 불경을 읽은 적은 없나요? Have you read any Buddhist sutras yet?

저는 《금강경》을 7년째 읽어오고 있습니다. I've been reading *the Diamond Sutra* for 7 years.

▶ 금강경 *Diamond Sutra* ▶ 반야심경 *Heart Sutra*

▶ 방해하다. **bother**

이런 식으로 방해하지 마세요. 집중할 수가 없군요. Don't bother me like this. I can't focus.

삼매에 들어가게 되면, 그 어떤 것도 마음을 방해하지 못할 겁니다. If you can enter into samadhi, nothing will bother your mind.

▶ 마음을 가라앉히다. **calm (your) mind**

마음을 가라앉히세요. Please be calm.

그 염불이 내 마음을 조용히 가라앉힌다. The chanting calms my mind.

차분히 마음을 가라앉히는 순간, 그의 마음은 맑은 물과 같다. When he keeps calm, his mind becomes like clear water.

▶ 〜이 들어 있다, (어떠한 내용물을)함유하고 있다. **contain**

그 땅콩버터에는 땅콩 말고는 아무것도 들어있지 않다. The peanut butter contains nothing but peanuts.

팔만대장경은 팔만사천 가지 부처님 말씀을 담고 있다. The *Tripitaka Koreana* contains 84,000 teachings of the Buddha.

Pair **W**ork Practice by substituting the underlined words with other proper words and phrases.

Sunim: What bothers you, Jackson?

Jackson: I worry about money and love.

Sunim: Reciting sutras will help you calm your mind.

Jackson: What sutra are you reading?

Sunim: I am reading the Heart Sutra.

Jackson: I want to read the Heart Sutra, too.

Sunim: It will take a long time.

5 참회

애나: 스님들도 속상할 때 화를 내나요?

스님: 스님들도 화를 낼 때가 있죠.

애나: 그래요? 어떤 경우인가요?

스님: 개인적인 욕심보다는 주로 다른 사람을 위해서 화를 낼 때가 있죠.
　　　설령 개인적인 일로 화가 나더라도 금방 참회를 한답니다.

애나: 참회요?

스님: 네. 금방 반성을 하고 다시 수행에 전념하지요.

Unit 5 Repentance

Anna:　Do monks get mad when something bad happens?

Sunim:　Monks sometimes get angry, too.

Anna:　Really? In what situations?

Sunim:　We usually get angry not for personal desires but for
the sake of others.
When we get angry over personal matters, we
immediately offer repentance.

Anna:　Offer repentance?

Sunim:　Yes. We immediately reflect on ourselves and focus
again on Buddhist practice.

▶ 화를 내다. **get mad (angry)**

당신은 화를 내본 적이 있습니까? Have you ever got mad? (Have you ever gotten mad? 미국에서만 사용)

그녀는 절대로 화를 안 냅니다. She never gets mad.

그녀가 그들에게 물을 쏟아버리자 그들은 몹시 화를 냈다. They got so mad after she threw the water at them.

▶ 경우 **situation**

이런 경우에는 좀더 인내심을 가지셔야 합니다. In this kind of situation, you should be more patient.

화두를 놓치면 수많은 상황이 당신의 마음을 방해할 수 있습니다. Any situations can disturb your mind if you don't keep your '*hwadu*'.

▶ 개인적인 욕심 **personal desires**

모든 중생들은 개개인의 욕망과 이기적인 잣대로 우리의 삶에서 고통받고 있습니다. All sentient beings suffer from personal desires and egoistic views of their lives.

그의 개인적인 포부는 유명한 예술가가 되는 것입니다. His personal desire is to become a famous artist.

▶ 개인적인 일 **personal matters**

사람들은 모두 개개인의 일로 늘 바쁘게 산다. People are busy all the time for their personal matters.

▶ ~위해서 **for the sake of**

나는 내 안의 평화를 위해서 계속 수행을 해야 한다. I should keep practicing for the sake of my inner-peace.

세계 평화를 위해서 전쟁은 그쳐야 한다. The war should be stopped for the sake of world peace.

그가 깊은 수행을 하도록 나는 그를 방해하지 않을 겁니다. I won't bother him for the sake of his deep practice.

▶ 참회 **offer repentance**

수행할 때는, 업을 정화하기 위해 반드시 부처님께 참회해야 한다. When one practices, one should offer repentance to the Buddha to purify one's *Karma*.

법당을 나가면서 나는 부처님께 참회하였다. On the way out of the Dharma hall, I offered repentance to the Buddha.

▶ 숙고하다. **reflect on**

참선과 절 수행은 잘못된 행동을 숙고하는 데 가장 좋은 수행방법 중 하나가 될 수 있다. Meditation and prostration practice can be the best way to reflect on one's bad deeds.

▶ 집중하다. **focus**

읽기에 집중이 되지 않는다. I can't focus on reading.

그는 요즘 절 수행에 한참입니다. He is focusing on prostration practice these days.

Pair Work   Practice by substituting the underlined words with other proper words and phrases.

Sunim:　When do you get mad, Anna?

Anna:　　I get mad when people hurt me.

Sunim:　For the sake of peace, you should offer repentance.

Anna:　　Personal matters make it hard for me to focus.

Sunim:　That's OK. Watch me and do as I do.

신수의 계송

身是菩提樹　몸은 보리수요,

心如明鏡臺　마음은 맑은 거울.

時時勤拂拭　늘 힘써 닦아

莫使有塵埃　티끌 묻지 않게 하라.

Shenxiu's Verse

The body is the bodhi tree,

The mind is like a clear mirror.

At all times you must strive to polish it

And must not let dust alight.

6 염불

애나: 스님! 지금 하시는 게 무엇인가요? 소리가 좋아요.

스님: '나무아미타불' 염불을 하고 있어요.

　　　염불은 마음을 한데 모으는 불교 수행입니다.

애나: '나무아미타불'은 무슨 의미인가요?

스님: 아미타불 부처님께 귀의한다는 뜻이지요.

애나: 다른 염불도 있나요?

스님: 한국에서는 '나무석가모니불' '나무관세음보살' 등도 염불합니다.

　　　티베트인들은 '옴마니 밧메 훔'을 많이 염불하지요.

Unit 6 Chanting

Anna: Sunim! What are you doing? I like the sound.

Sunim: I am chanting '*Namu Amitabul.*' Chanting is a
Buddhist practice. It helps me to concentrate.

Anna: What does '*Namu Amitabul*' mean?

Sunim: It means: "I pay homage to Amitabha Buddha."

Anna: Are there any other kinds of chanting?

Sunim: In Korea, we also chant 'Homage to Sakyamuni
Buddha' or 'Homage to Avalokitesvara Bodhisattva.'
Tibetans often chant '*Om mani padme hum.*'

▶ 무슨 의미입니까? **What do/does ~ mean?**

그게 무슨 말인가요? What do you mean?

'해우소' 라는 것은 무슨 의미죠? What does '*Haeuso*' mean?

미안하지만 당신이 지금 한 말을 알아듣지 못하겠어요. I'm sorry but I don't understand what you just said.

▶ 염불, 염불하다. **chant**

▶ 염불하기 **chanting**

▶ 귀의하다. **take refuge in, pay homage to**

삼귀의(三歸依): The Three Refuges.

I take refuge in the Buddha

I take refuge in the Dharma

I take refuge in the Sangha.

▶ 마음을 한데 모으다, 집중하다. **concentrate (on)**

초보자라면 처음에 참선을 할때 천천히 호흡에 집중을 하도록 해보세요. When you meditate, you should concentrate on slow breathing at first, if you are a beginner.

▶ 나무아미타불 **Namu Amitabul: (I pay) homage to Amitabha Buddha**

나무관세음보살 Namu Gwanseumbosal: (I pay) homage to Avalokitesvara Bodhisatva

나무석가모니불 Namu Seokgamonibul: (I pay) homage to Sakyamuni Buddha

▶ 종류 **kind**

얼마나 많은 불경이 거기에 있습니까? How many kinds of Buddhist sutras are there?

이런 일은 어려워요(쉽지 않군요.) This kind of work is not so easy.

그런 냄새를 정말 좋아합니다. I love that kind of smell.

Pair Work Practice by substituting the underlined words with other proper words and phrases.

Anna: Why do you chant?

Sunim: I chant because it helps me to concentrate.

Anna: What kind of chant is it?

Sunim: I am chanting "*Namu Gwanseeumbosal.*"

Anna: What does it mean?

Sunim: It means "I pay homage to Avalokitesvara

7 계율

(더운 여름날, 모기에 물린 마틴이 팔을 긁고 있다.)
마틴: 스님들은 모기도 잡지 않나요?
스님: (웃으며) 스님들은 작은 생명도 소중히 합니다.
마틴: 그럼 모기들은 어떻게 하지요?
스님: 청소를 깨끗이 하고, 방충망을 쳐서 되도록 들어오지 못하게 하지요.
마틴: (난처해하며) 모기를 잡는 것은 불교정신에 어긋나는 것이겠네요.
스님: 그렇죠. 불교 계율에 어긋납니다.

Unit 7 Buddhist Precepts

(On a hot summer day, Martin is scratching a mosquito bite on his arm.)

Martin: Do monks not even kill mosquitoes?

Sunim: (laughing) Monks value even the smallest living things.

Martin: Then what do you do about mosquitoes?

Sunim: We clean a lot and try our best to keep them outside with bug screens.

Martin: (Embarrassed) Then killing mosquitoes violates the spirit of Buddhism.

Sunim: That's correct. It violates the precepts of Buddhism.

▶ 모기 **mosquito (mosquitoes)**

여름철에는 산속에 모기들이 몹시 많아요. There are so many mosquitoes in the mountain during summer time.

이곳은 매우 춥고 건조해서 모기가 없어요. We don't have any mosquitoes here since it is very dry and cold.

▶ 파리 **fly / flies**

우리는 파리 몇 마리가 방에서 날아다니는 것을 보았다. We saw some flies flying in the room.

그 파리는 땀이 흐르는 스님의 머리 위에 앉아 있었다. The fly was sitting on the monk's sweating head.

▶ ~조차도 **not even ~**

나는 저녁 먹으러 가는 것조차도 생각하고 있지 않습니다. I'm not even thinking about going out for dinner.

그는 내 이름조차도 알고 있지 않아요. He doesn't even know my name.

▶ 소중히 하다. **value**

물질주의는 정신주의를 그리 소중히 생각하지 않습니다. Materialism doesn't value spirituality much.

▶ 최선을 다하다, 애쓰다. **do/try (one's) best**

최선을 다하십시오. 그러면 후회하지 않을 겁니다. Do your best so that you don't regret.

최선을 다하세요. Why don't you do your best?

▶ ~정신에 어긋나다. **violate the spirit of~**

그것은 수행의 정신에 어긋나는 것입니다. It violates the spirit of practice.

그 어떤 것도 우리 문화의 정신을 파괴시킬 수 없습니다. Nothing can violate the spirit of our culture.

▶ ~계율에 어긋나다. **violate the precepts**

계율을 어기면 문제가 생길 거에요. If you violate the precepts, you will be in trouble.

▶ 긁다. **scratch**

모기에 물린 후 긁지 마세요. 그렇지 않으면 더 악화됩니다. Don't scratch after a mosquito bites you. It will get worse otherwise.

그는 무슨 말을 할 때 부끄러우면 머리를 긁적입니다. He scratches his head whenever he feels shy about saying something.

Practice by substituting the underlined words with other proper words and phrases.

Sunim: Why are you scratching your arm?

Martin: A fly bit me. Is it OK to kill flies?

Sunim: Killing violates the precepts of Buddhism.

Martin: I will try my best not to kill flies.

Sunim: Buddhists value all life, so you must not kill any creature, not even a fly.

Martin: Yes, Sunim!

혜능의 계송

菩提本無樹　　보리나무 본래 없고

明鏡亦非臺　　거울 또한 틀이 아니네.

佛性常淸淨　　불성은 늘 청정한데

何處有塵埃　　어디에 먼지 있으리.

Huineng's Verse

Bodhi originally has no tree.

The bright mirror also has no stand.

Since Buddha nature is always pure,

Where could dust alight?

Chapter 6 Korean Buddhist History and Culture 한국불교 역사와 문화

1 대한불교조계종

마틴: 한국불교에는 스님들이 다 같은 종파인가요?

스님: 아닙니다. 한국에는 여러 개의 종파가 나누어져 있답니다.

마틴: 그럼 스님은 무슨 종인가요?

스님: 저는 대한불교조계종 스님입니다.

마틴: 대한불교조계종 스님은 많은가요?

스님: 물론입니다. 한국불교를 대표하는 종단이니까요.

마틴: 제가 제대로 찾아왔군요.

Unit 1 The Jogye Order of Korean Buddhism

Martin: Do all Korean monks belong to the same Buddhist Order?

Sunim: No. Korean Buddhism is divided into several orders.

Martin: Sunim! What order do you belong to?

Sunim: I am a monk from the Jogye Order of Korean Buddhism.

Martin: Are there many monks in the Jogye Order of Korean Buddhism?

Sunim: Of course, because it is the representative order of Korean Buddhism.

Martin: I see I've come to the right place.

Words & Phrases

▶ 종 **Order**

조계종은 한국불교에서 가장 큰 종입니다. Jogye Order is the biggest order in Korean Buddhism.

▶ ~에 속하다. **belong to**

저는 조계종 소속입니다. I belong to the Jogye Order.

이 도서관은 이 대학교에 속해 있어요. This library belongs to the University.

▶ 종교 **religion**

모든 종교는 평화에 대해 말한다. All religions talk about peace.

당신의 종교가 무엇입니까? What is your religion?

Cf. 신앙심이 있는 분이신가요(종교생활을 하시는 분입니까?) Are you religious?

▶ (기독교의) 종파 **denomination**

기독교는 수백 개의 종파로 나뉘어져 있다. Christianity is divided into hundreds of denominations.

▶ 감리교 **Methodist**

▶ 침례교 **Baptist**

▶ 고기를 먹다. **eat meat**

죄송하지만, 제가 채식주의자라 고기를 먹을 수 없습니다. I'm sorry I can't eat meat because I'm a vegetarian.

고기를 먹는 것은 계율에 어긋납니다. Eating meat violates the precepts of monastic life.

Pair Work Practice by substituting the underlined words with other proper words.

Sunim: Do you have a religion?

Martin: My parents are Methodist. Does Buddhism have different denominations, too?

Sunim: Yes, Buddhism has different orders. They are similar to Christian denominations.

Martin: What are the differences among Buddhist Orders?

Sunim: Some orders allow monks to marry.

Martin: That is similar to some Christian denominations, too.

2 불교 역사

잭슨: 불교의 역사는 얼마나 오래 되었나요?

스님: 부처님 당시로부터 2600년쯤 되었습니다.

잭슨: 그럼 한국불교는 얼마나 되었나요?

스님: 한국불교는 1700년의 역사를 가지고 있습니다.

잭슨: 와우, 정말 긴 역사를 가졌군요.

Unit 2 History of Buddhism

Jackson: How long is Buddhist history?

Sunim: It has been about twenty-six hundred years since the time of the Buddha.

Jackson: Then how old is Korean Buddhism?

Sunim: Korean Buddhism has seventeen hundred years of history.

Jackson: Wow, that's a really long time.

▶ ~이 얼마나 길어요 **How long**

그 회기는 기간이 얼마인가요? How long is the session?

얼마나 오래 참선을 하셔요? How long do you do meditation?

▶ ~ 이래로 **since ~**

나는 한국문화에 매료된 후 계속 한국에서 살아오고 있답니다. I've been in Korea since I fell in love with Korean culture.

▶ ~년의 역사를 가지다. **have ~ years of history**

한국은 6000년이 넘는 역사를 가지고 있습니다. Korea has more than six thousand years of history.

우리 사찰은 300년의 역사를 가지고 있습니다. Our temple has three hundred years of history.

▶ 긴 시간, 오랜 시간, 긴 역사 **a long time**

오랜만에 뵙습니다. It's been a long time since we met you.

그 절에 가는 데 오래 걸리지는 않습니다. It doesn't take a long time to get to the temple.

▶ 대략 **about**

그는 미국에 한 5년 전에 갔었지요. He went to the United States about 5 years ago.

나는 이곳에 약 9년 동안 있었습니다. I've been here for about 9 years.

Pair Work Practice by substituting the underlined words with other proper words and phrases.

Sunim: Jackson, how long have you been in Korea?

Jackson: I have been in Seoul since last Monday.

Sunim: Where are you from?

Jackson: I'm from the U.S.

Sunim: How long is the history of the United States?

Jackson: About 240 years.

3 성도재일

스님: 내일은 부처님 성도재일입니다. 그래서 오늘 밤에 정진이 있습니다.
7시까지 큰방으로 오세요.

잭슨: 성도재일이 뭔가요?

스님: 성도재일은 부처님께서 깨달으신 날을 기념하는 것입니다.

잭슨: 그런데 왜 밤에 정진을 하죠?

스님: 부처님 성도하신 것을 기념해야죠. 오늘만큼은 우리도 정진을 통해
부처님께서 깨달으신 의미를 되새기기 위해서랍니다.

잭슨: 그럼 모두 큰방에 모여서 좌선을 하는 건가요?

스님: 네, 일단은 좌선을 하고요. 졸리면 절 수행을 하셔도 좋습니다.

Unit 3 Bodhi Day

Sunim: Tomorrow is Buddha's Bodhi Day. That's why tonight
we have a special Buddhist practice. Please come to
the Great Hall by 7 o'clock.

Jackson: What's Bodhi Day?

Sunim: Bodhi Day marks the day when the Buddha attained
Enlightenment.

Jackson: Then why do you have to practice at night?

Sunim: We must commemorate Buddha's enlightenment. On a
day like today we must focus on Buddhist practice and
reflect on the meaning of Buddha's enlightenment.

Jackson: So everyone will gather in the Great Hall and do
sitting meditation?

Sunim: Yes, first we will do sitting meditation. If you get
drowsy, you may perform prostration practice.

▶ ~시까지 오세요. **come by ~o'clock**

그 표를 예약하고 싶으시면, 사무실에 오후 5시까지 오세요. If you'd like to book the ticket, please come to the office by 5 pm.

내일 아침 10시까지 돌아오세요. Come back by 10 o'clock in the morning(10 am).

▶ 기념하다, (기억하기 위해) 표시해두다. **mark(s)**

그는 성도재일을 기억하기 위해 달력에 표시를 하였다. He marked Bodhi Day on the calendar to remember.

나는 그녀의 생일을 내 일기장에 표시해두었다. I marked her birthday in my diary.

▶ 깨달음을 이루다, 깨달음을 얻다. **attain enlightenment**

깨달음을 이룬다는 것은 쉽지 않다. It's not easy to attain enlightenment.

▶ 기념하다. **commemorate**

모든 불자들은 매년 부처님오신날에 부처님의 가르침을 기리고 있다. All Buddhists commemorate the Buddha's teaching on the Buddha's Birthday every year.

우리는 우리 선원 은사님의 입적 1주년 기념 행사를 하였다. We commemorated our Seon Master's 1-year anniversary after he passed away.

▶ 졸리다. **get drowsy / sleepy**

졸려서 낮잠을 좀 자야겠어요. I should take a nap because I feel so sleepy.

약을 먹고 나니 졸리군요. I feel drowsy from the medicine I took.

▶ 절 수행 **prostration practice**　　　▶ 부처님오신날 **Buddha's Birthday**

Pair Work　Practice by substituting the underlined words with other proper words and phrases.

Sunim:　Tomorrow is Buddha's Birthday.

Jackson: What's Buddha's Birthday?

Sunim:　Buddha's Birthday marks the day when Buddha came into the world.

Jackson: Is that why many people are gathering in the temple?

Sunim:　Yes, people gather to commemorate the coming of the Buddha.

Jackson: How can I commemorate the coming of the Buddha?

Sunim:　By prostration. Here, do as I do.

Jackson: Yes, Sunim!

4 법랍

애나: 스님들 사이에도 서열이 있나요?

스님: 네, 스님들 사이에는 서열이 있습니다.

애나: 어떤 서열이죠? 연령인가요?

스님: 아닙니다. 스님들은 먼저 출가하신 분을 윗사람으로 받듭니다.

애나: 그것을 가리키는 말이 따로 있나요?

스님: 네, 스님들의 출가서열을 법랍이라고 합니다.

애나: 그러면 스님의 법랍은 얼마인가요?

스님: 저는 출가한 지 10년이 되었답니다. 그러니까 제 법랍은 10년이지요.

Unit 4 Dharma Age

Anna: Is there rank even among monks?

Sunim: Yes, there is rank even among monks.

Anna: What kind of ranking system is it? Is it by age?

Sunim: No. Those who entered the order first are considered senior.

Anna: Is there a word that explains this rank?

Sunim: Yes, a monk's Dharma age shows their rank.

Anna: Then what is your Dharma age?

Sunim: It has been 10 years since I was ordained, so my Dharma age is 10 years.

▶ 서열 **rank, ranking system**

그는 우리의 절에서 가장 지위가 높은 분이다. He has the highest rank in our monastery.

▶ ~사이에, 중에 **among ~**

이 경전은 부처님의 가르침을 배우기에 가장 쉬운 것으로, 초급자에게 좋다. This sutra is the easiest one for beginners to understand the Buddha's teachings.

그는 그 그룹 사람들 가운데 가장 부자이다. He's the richest man among the people in the group.

그녀는 그 교실의 학생들 중에서 가장 똑똑하다. She is the best student among all the students in the class.

▶ 연령별로 **by age**

그 문서들은 연령별로 분류되어 있다. The documents were sorted by age.

연령별로 정리가 된 그 파일을 섞지 마세요. Please don't mix the file arranged by age.

▶ 출가하다. **enter the order, renounce secular life, leave home to become a monk**

일단 출가를 하면, 열심히 수행을 해서 깨달음을 얻도록 하라. Once you enter the order, keep practicing hard so that you can reach enlightenment.

출가하려는 결심은 모든 사람이 할 수 있는 일은 아니다. It's not for everybody to decide to enter an order of Buddhism.

▶ 윗사람 **senior**

그 일은 선배스님과 상의해야 한다. You should check with a senior monk about that.

그 일은 선임연구원에게 물어보세요. Consult with the senior researcher about that.

▶ 설명하다. **explain**

그가 한국불교를 위해 한 업적에 대해 말씀해주세요. Please explain to me what he's done for developing Buddhism in Korea.

그가 나보다 더 잘 설명할 수 있습니다. He can explain better than me.

▶ 법랍 **Dharma age**

내 법랍은 겨우 10년밖에 되지 못했다. My Dharma age is only 10 years.

아무도 그의 법랍을 알지 못한다. Nobody knows his Dharma age.

▶ 스님이 되다, 계를 받다. **be ordained**

그는 10년 전에 스님이 되셨습니다. He was ordained 10 years ago.

그녀는 사흘 후에 계를 받을 겁니다. She will be ordained in 3 days.

▶ 주지스님 **abbot, abbess**

▶ 행자 **monastic trainee / postulant.**

▶ 가장 높은 **(the) highest** / 가장 낮은 **(the) lowest**

▶ 동등한 **equal**

모든 인간은 동등하다. All humans are equal.

민주정치는 사람들이 사회활동을 하는 데 동등한 기회를 준다. Democracy gives people an equal chance at social activities.

▶ 정하다. **determine**

그들은 다음날 아침 일찍 출발하기로 결정했다. They determined to start early the next day.

우승자는 심사위원회에서 정할 것이다. The winner will be determined by the selection committee.

Pair Work Practice by substituting the underlined words with other proper words.

Anna:　Who has the highest rank in the temple?

Sunim:　The abbot has the highest rank in the temple?

Anna:　How do you determine rank?

Sunim:　Dharma age determines rank.

Anna:　What is your Dharma age, Sunim?

Sunim:　My Dharma age is 15 years.

칭찬과 비난

이득과 손실

즐거움과 슬픔은

바람처럼 가고 오는 것

행복을 원한다면

그런 팔풍 속에서 거목처럼 평온하라.

Praise and blame

gain and loss

pleasure and sorrow

come and go like the wind

To be happy, rest like a great tree

in the midst of them all.

- The Buddha

5 승복

애나: 스님, 한국 스님들은 왜 회색 옷만 입나요?

스님: 검소함의 상징으로 먹물 들인 옷을 입는 겁니다.

애나: 이런 옷을 뭐라고 하나요?

스님: 승복이라고 합니다.

애나: 스님들은 항상 이 옷만 입나요?

스님: 네, 늘 승복을 입고 생활합니다.

애나: 왜 이 옷만 입어야 하는 거죠?

스님: 승복은 출가자로서의 본분을 지키기 위해 입는 옷이기 때문입니다.

Unit 5 Monastic Robes

Anna: Sunim! Why do Korean monks only wear gray robes?

Sunim: We only wear clothes dyed with Chinese ink to live simply.

Anna: What do you call these clothes?

Sunim: They are called '*seungbok*', or monastic robes.

Anna: Do monks always wear them?

Sunim: Yes, they wear these robes in everyday life.

Anna: Why must monks only wear these clothes?

Sunim: Monastic robes help them remember their duty as renunciant monks.

▶ 승복 **(monastic) robe**

승복이 보통 얼마하나요? How much is the monastic robe in general?

그는 승복이 잘 어울린다. Monastic robes suit him well.

▶ 염색하다. **dye**

머리를 염색한다는 것은 건강에 좋지 않아요! Dyeing hair is not good for your health.

이 옷들은 비화학 염색재로 염색된 것이다. These clothes were dyed with non-chemical dyeing materials.

▶ 검소하게 살다. **live simply**

검소하게 사는 것은 당신의 삶을 평화롭게 하는 가장 최상의 방법이다. If you live simply, that's the best way to make your life peaceful.

스님들은 검소하게 사신다. Monks and nuns live simply.

▶ 일상생활 **everyday life**

▶ 본분 **duty**

▶ 출가자 **renunciant monk**

▶ 만약 **if**

내게 돈이 있다면, 나는 여행을 갈 것이다. If I have some money, I will go traveling.

만일 그녀가 요리를 한다면, 우리는 그녀를 이 절에 고용하겠다. If she cooks, we'll hire her for this temple.

Pair Work Practice by substituting the underlined words with other proper words.

Anna: Sunim, can I wear monastic robes, too?

Sunim: If you become a monastic trainee, you can wear monastic robes, too.

Anna: How can I become a monastic trainee?

Sunim: To become a monastic trainee, you must renounce the secular life.

Anna: Can I live simply without becoming a monastic trainee?

Sunim: Yes, you can if you do Buddhist practice.

6 녹차

(녹차를 내며)

스님: 이런 차는 처음 마셔보죠?

마틴: 네, 스님.

스님: 차 맛이 어떻습니까?

마틴: 향이 아주 좋아요. 이 차 이름은 뭡니까?

스님: 이것은 한국에서 나는 녹차입니다. 일본 녹차와는 맛이 아주 다르지요.

마틴: 아 그렇군요. 찻잔도 너무 예뻐요.

(스님이 한 잔 더 따라준다)

마틴: 또 마셔요?

스님: 녹차는 보통 세 잔까지 마신답니다.

Unit 6 Green Tea

(The monk gives Martin a cup of green tea)

Sunim: Is this your first time drinking tea like this?

Martin: Yes, Sunim.

Sunim: How does the tea taste?

Martin: It has a good aroma. What do you call this tea?

Sunim: This is green tea grown in Korea. It tastes quite different from Japanese green tea.

Martin: Oh really. The teacup is also very pretty.

(Sunim pours Martin another cup of tea)

Martin: Drink again?

Sunim: We usually drink up to three cups of green tea at one sitting.

Words & Phrases

▶ 녹차 **green tea**

나는 녹차를 거의 매일 마신다. I drink green tea almost every day.

녹차나 홍차를 마시겠습니까? Would you like to drink green tea or black tea?

▶ 처음 **first time**

▶ ~ 맛이 어떻습니까? **"How does ~ taste?"** 또는 **"What does ~ taste like?"**

김치 맛이 어떤가요? What does *kimchi* taste like?

사찰 음식 맛이 어땠어요? How did you like the taste of the temple food?

▶ 향 **aroma**

그 향의 향내가 꽤 독하군요. The aroma of the incense is rather strong!

이 차의 향이 아주 좋군요. I like the smell of this tea very much. 또는 This tea has a very nice fragrance.

▶ 찻잔 **teacup**

몇 개의 찻잔이 필요합니까? How many teacups do you need?

다섯 개 필요해요. I need five cups.

▶ 붓다 **pour**

차 주전자에 너무 물을 많이 붓지 마세요. Don't pour too much water into the tea pot.

제 컵에 차 좀 따라주세요. Please pour some tea into my cup.

▶ 한 자리에 **at one sitting**　　▶ 연잎차 **Lotus leaf tea**

▶ 자스민차 **Jasmine tea**　　▶ 진정시키다. **soothe, calm**

참선은 사람의 마음을 진정시켜줄 수 있다. Meditation can soothe one's mind.

차를 마시는 것은 사람의 마음을 편안하게 해주는 한 방법이다. Drinking tea is the way of soothing one's spirit.

▶ 대만 **Taiwan**

Pair Work Practice by substituting the underlined words with other proper words and phrases.

Sunim: How <u>does</u> the tea <u>taste</u>?

Martin: It is very <u>soothing</u>. What do you call this tea?

Sunim: This is <u>lotus leaf tea</u> grown in <u>Taiwan</u>. It tastes <u>quite different from green tea</u>.

Martin: I like it!

Sunim: Would you like another cup?

Martin: <u>Yes, please.</u>

Chapter 7 One-Line Expressions 한 줄 표현

Unit 1 Greetings 인사 표현

처음 뵙겠습니다. 저는 법민 스님입니다.	How do you do? I'm Beobmin Sunim.
당신을 어떻게 부르면 되겠습니까?	How do I address you?
스님이라고 부르세요.	Please call me Sunim.
만나서 반갑습니다.	Nice to meet you.
알게 되어 기쁩니다.	Nice to meet you / It's a pleasure to meet you.
이름이 어떻게 되죠?	What's your name?
제 이름은 애나입니다.	My name is Anna.
어디서 오셨습니까?	Where are you from?
캐나다에서 왔어요.	I'm from Canada.
어느 나라 분이십니까?	What is your nationality?
저는 캐나다 사람입니다.	I'm Canadian.
제 소개를 하겠습니다.	Allow me to introduce myself.
안녕하세요. 저는 존입니다.	Hello, I'm John.
저는 미국에서 왔습니다.	I'm from the United States.
두 분이 서로 인사를 나누셨습니까?	Have you two introduced yourselves?
아니요. / 예, 인사했어요.	No, we haven't. / Yes, we have.
제 친구인 마틴을 소개하겠습니다.	Let me introduce my friend Martin to you.
서로 좋은 친구가 되었으면 합니다.	I hope you become good friends.
만나서 반가웠습니다.	It was a pleasure meeting you.
또 만납시다.	We'll meet again.

다음에 뵙겠습니다.	See you next time.
가끔 연락하며 지내요.	Let's keep in touch.
연락드리겠습니다.	I'll contact you.
가끔 전화주세요.	Give me a call once in a while.
멋진 여행이 되길 바랍니다.	I hope you have a wonderful trip.
친절을 베풀어주셔서 감사합니다.	Thank you for your hospitality.
신세가 많았습니다.	I am indebted to you.
당신과 멋진 시간을 보냈습니다.	I had a wonderful time with you.
저희 절을 방문해 주셔서 감사합니다.	Thank you for visiting our temple.
별말씀을요.	You're welcome / Don't mention it. / No problem.
맛있게 드셨다니 다행입니다.	I'm glad you enjoyed the food.
늦어서 죄송합니다.	Forgive me for being late.
부처님오신날을 축하합니다.	Happy Buddha's Birthday!
한국에 오신 것을 환영합니다.	Welcome to Korea.
우리 절에 오신 것을 환영합니다.	Welcome to our temple.
이곳이 마음에 들기를 바랍니다.	I hope you like it here.

2 사찰 일상표현

Expressions for Everyday Temple Life

저는 템플스테이 담당자입니다.	I'm the Templestay program director.
저는 이곳 원주스님입니다.	I am this temple's proctor.
이분은 이 절 주지스님입니다.	This is the Abbot of our temple.
여기에 성함을 써주세요.	Please sign in here.
이 서류를 작성해주세요.	Please fill out this form.
저희 사찰은 처음인가요?	Is this your first time at our temple?
네, 처음이에요 / 아니요, 전에 왔었어요.	Yes, it is. / No, it isn't. I've visited before.
한국은 처음인가요?	Is this your first time in Korea?
네, 그래요. / 아니요, 온 적이 있어요.	Yes, it is. / No, it isn't. I've visited before.
템플스테이는 처음인가요?	Is this your first Templestay?
네, 그래요. / 아니요, 해 본 적 있어요.	Yes, it is. / No, it isn't. I've experienced a Templestay before.
템플스테이 기간은 3일부터 8일까지입니다.	The Templestay is from the third to the eighth of the month.
템플스테이는 15일부터 시작합니다.	The Templestay will start on the fifteenth (of the month).
템플스테이는 20일에 끝납니다.	The Templestay will end on the twentieth (of the month).
이곳은 대웅전입니다.	This is the Main Buddha Hall.
이곳은 관음전입니다.	This is the Avalokitesvara Hall.
이곳은 지장전입니다.	This is the Hall of the Earth-store Bodhisattva.
이곳은 종각입니다.	This is the Bell Pavilion.
절에서는 금언입니다.	The entire temple is non-smoking.
잠깐 들어오십시오.	Please come in for a moment.

이쪽으로 오십시오.	This way, please.
객실은 스스로 청소해야 합니다.	Participants must clean their own rooms.
예불은 몇 시에 합니까?	When is the Buddhist ceremony?
＿＿＿시에 합니다.	It is at ＿＿＿ am/pm?
공양은 몇 시에 하나요?	When is mealtime?
기상시간은 몇 시인가요?	When is wakeup time?
취침시간은 몇 시인가요?	When is bedtime?
잠은 어디에서 자나요?	Where do I sleep?
저 방에서 주무시면 됩니다.	You will sleep in that room.
공양은 어디에서 하나요?	Where do we eat meals?
공양간에서 합니다.	We eat meals in the refectory.
내일은 4시에 예불을 합니다.	The morning ceremony is at 4:00 am tomorrow.
내일 기상시간은 3시 50분입니다.	Wakeup time tomorrow is 3:50 am.
점심공양은 발우공양으로 합니다.	Lunch will be baru gongyang, the formal monastic meal.
아침공양은 공양간에서 합니다.	You can have breakfast in the refectory.
해우소는 어느 쪽으로 가죠?	Which way is the restroom (toilet)?
(가리키며) 저쪽으로 직진하다 오른쪽(왼쪽)으로 가세요.	(pointing) Go straight that way and make a right / left.
종각은 어느 쪽인가요?	Which way is the Bell Pavilion?
(가리키며) 저쪽으로 가세요.	(pointing) Go that way.
법당은 어느 쪽입니까?	Which way is the Dharma hall?
오늘은 부처님오신날입니다.	Today is Buddha's Birthday.
내일은 열반재일입니다.	Tomorrow is Nirvana Day, the day the Buddha entered parinirvana.
대한불교조계종은 한국불교를 대표합니다.	The Jogye Order represents Korean Buddhism.

한국불교는 1700년의 역사를 가지고 있습니다.	Korean Buddhism has seventeen hundred years of history.
이 탑은 신라시대에 조성되었습니다.	This pagoda was built during the Silla Dynasty.
우리 절은 고려시대에 세워졌습니다.	This temple was built during the Goryeo Dynasty.
이 절은 조선시대에 세워졌습니다.	This temple was built during the Joseon Dynasty.
원효 스님이 세운 절입니다.	The Venerable Wonhyo founded this temple.
의상 스님이 세운 절입니다.	The Venerable Uisang founded this temple.
절하는 법을 가르쳐 드리겠습니다.	I'll teach you how to prostrate.
발우공양하는 법을 가르쳐 드리겠습니다.	I'll teach you how to perform baru gongyang, the formal monastic meal.
따라해 보십시오.	Please do as I do.
저를 따라 오세요.	Please follow behind me.
새벽 예불에 참석하세요.	Please join us for the early morning ceremony.
저녁 예불에 참석하세요.	Please join us for the evening ceremony.
도량안내를 해드리겠습니다.	Let me show you around the temple.
마실 것을 좀 드릴까요?	Can I get you something to drink?
네, 좋아요. / 아니, 괜찮아요.	Yes, please. / No, thank you.
공양 하셨습니까?	Have you eaten?
예, 먹었습니다. / 아니요.	Yes, I have. / No, I haven't.
이것은 녹차입니다.	This is green tea.
이것은 보이차입니다.	This is Bo-ee tea (Puer tea, dark fermented green tea).
지리산에서 만든 차입니다.	This tea was made on Jiri Mountain.
절 하니까 어떠세요?	How do you feel after prostration practice?

다리가 아프네요.	My legs are sore.
절하는 것이 힘들지는 않나요?	Isn't prostration difficult?
힘들어요. / 아니요.	Yes, it is. / No, it isn't.
참선하는 게 힘들지 않나요?	Isn't Seon meditation difficult?
사찰음식이 입에 맞나요?	How is temple food?
좋아요, 괜찮아요, 좋지 않아요?	It's good. / It's OK. / I don't like it.
사찰 분위기가 어떤가요?	How is the temple ambiance?
평화롭네요.	It's peaceful.
한국불교를 어떻게 생각하나요?	What do you think about Korean Buddhism?
훌륭해요.	I think it's fascinating.
한국 스님들을 어떻게 생각하나요?	What do you think about Korean monks?
헌신적이십니다.	I think they are very dedicated.
템플스테이를 하고 난 소감을 말해 보세요.	Please share your thoughts about having experienced the Templestay.
전혀 새로운 체험이었어요.	It was a totally new experience for me.
예불한 소감을 말해 보세요.	Please share your thoughts about having experienced the Buddhist ceremony.
마음이 고요했습니다.	It was very calming.

Part 2

Buddhist Tenets
불교 교리

1 불교란 무엇인가?

불교는 정신적 발전을 위한 길이다.

불교는 부처님의 가르침을 근간으로 하고 있다.

불교는 실재의 본성을 깨치도록 도와준다.

불교는 실재를 있는 그대로 볼 수 있게 해준다.

불교는 고통을 멸하고 행복을 키울 수 있게 해준다.

불교는 창조주 신을 숭배하지 않는다.

불교는 명상 등의 정신적 발전을 이룰 수 있는 수단을 제공한다.

불교 수행은 깨어있음, 자애, 지혜를 닦을 수 있게 해준다.

Unit 1 What is Buddhism?

Buddhism is a path of spiritual development.

Buddhism is based on the teachings of the Buddha.

Buddhism helps us awaken to the true nature of reality.

Buddhism helps us see reality as it is.

Buddhism helps us overcome suffering and attain happiness.

Buddhism does not worship a creator god.

Buddhism provides a means of spiritual development through practices like meditation.

Buddhist practices help us develop mindfulness, kindness, and wisdom.

Buddhism is a _____ of spiritual development. (길)

Buddhism is based on the _____ of the Buddha. (가르침)

Buddhism helps us awaken to the _____ of reality. (참모습)

Buddhism helps us see _____ as it is. (실재)

Buddhism helps us overcome _____ and attain happiness. (고)

Buddhism does not _____ a creator god. (숭배하다)

Buddhism provides a means of spiritual development like _____. (명상)

Buddhist practices help us develop _____, kindness, and wisdom.

(깨어있음, 정념)

Buddhism is a path of spiritual development.

Questions

1. Is Buddhism based on the teachings of Rahula?

2. Does Buddhism help us overcome happiness?

3. Does Buddhism help us develop mindfulness?

4. How does Buddhism help us awaken?

5. Is Buddhism a path?

6. Do you follow the path of Buddhism?

7. Do you meditate?

How does Buddhism help us awaken?

2 부처님 생애

부처님은 네팔의 사캬족 왕자, 싯다르타 고타마로 태어났다. 기원전 566년 왕자가 29세가 되었을 때 고통에서 자유로워질 수 있는 길을 찾아 집을 떠났다. 6년간의 힘겨운 고행 끝에 싯다르타는 고행을 버리고 보리수나무 아래서 명상에 들었다.

어느 날 샛별이 떠오를 때 싯다르타는 깨달음을 얻은 이, 부처가 되었다.

부처님은 그 후로도 45년간이나 북인도 평원을 다니며 자신이 깨달은 '도' 즉 법을 가르쳤다. 부처님은 가르침을 실천하는 스님들이 대중살이하는 교단을 구성하셨다. 즉 비구 승가가 생겼고 뒤이어 비구니 승가도 생겼다. 기원전 486년경 부처님은 80세로 돌아가셨다. 마지막으로 남긴 말씀은 다음과 같다.

모든 복합된 존재는 허망하나니
부지런히 닦아 해탈에 힘쓸지니.

 The Life of the Buddha

The Buddha was born Siddhartha Gautama, a prince of the Sakya clan of what we now call Nepal, in approximately 566 BCE. When he was 29 years old, he left home to find a way to be free from suffering. After six years of severe ascetic practices, he abandoned the way of self-mortification, and instead, sat in meditation beneath a bodhi tree. One day, with the rising of the morning star, Siddhartha Gautama became the Buddha, the enlightened one.

The Buddha wandered the plains of northeastern India for 45 more years, teaching the path, or Dharma, he had realized. He developed a monastic community for the communal living of Buddhist practitioners; first the Sangha of monks and, later, nuns. In approximately 486 BCE, at the age of 80, the Buddha passed away. His last words were:

All composite things are impermanent.
Strive for your own liberation with diligence.

The Buddha was born a prince of the _____ _____ . (샤카족)

He left home to find a way to be _____ _____ suffering. (자유로운)

After six years of severe _____ _____ . (고행)

He sat in meditation beneath a _____ _____ . (보리수)

Siddhartha Gautama became the Buddha, the _____ _____ .

(깨달은 사람)

The Buddha taught the path or _____ he had realized. (다르마)

He developed a monastic community for _____ _____ . (대중살이)

At the age of 80, the Buddha _____ _____ . (돌아가시다)

All composite things are _____ . (무상한)

Strive for your own _____ with diligence. (해탈)

1. What was the name of the Buddha when he was a child?

2. Was Siddhartha a prince of the Magadha Kingdom?

3. When was Siddhartha born?

4. How old was Siddhartha when he left home?

5. What does the word "Buddha" mean?

6. How long did the Buddha teach?

7. Did the Buddha develop the community of Buddhist nuns first?

3 승가

산스크리트어 '상가(Sangha)'에는 두 가지 의미가 있다. 넓은 의미로는 '사부대중'이고 좁은 의미로는 계를 받은 스님들의 집단을 의미한다. 여기서는 후자의 의미인 승가를 설명하겠다. 부처님은 많은 사람들에게 불교수행자가 가야 할 길에서 벗어나지 않을 수 있는 방법을 말씀하셨다. 그것은 도반이 있는 것, 즉 '승가'라 불리는 도반의 집단과 함께 하는 것이다. 승가의 중요성은 《절반경》에 잘 설명되어 있다.

아난다가 부처님께 말했다.
"좋은 벗은 청정범행의 절반입니다, 세존이시여."
부처님이 답하셨다.
"그렇지 않다. 좋은 벗은 실은 청정범행의 전부이다. 비구에게 좋은 벗이 있을 때… 그는 팔정도를 잘 닦고 실천할 수 있다."

Unit 3 **The Sangha**

"Sangha" has two meanings: the fourfold community in a wider sense and the Buddhist community of ordained monks and nuns in a narrower sense. Here, we will focus on the latter.
The Buddha advised many people on ways to avoid being distracted from following the spiritual path. One was to have spiritual friends, i.e. a group of spiritual friends named the Sangha.
The Sangha's importance is explained in the *Upaddha Sutta*.

Ven. Ananda said to the Buddha,
"This is half of the holy life, World-Honored-One, admirable friendship."
The Buddha replied, "Don't say that. Admirable friendship is actually the whole of the holy life. When a monk has admirable people as friends ... he can be expected to develop and practice the Noble Eightfold Path."

Fill in the Blanks

The _____ _____ in a wider sense. (사부대중)

The Buddhist community of _____ monks and nuns in a narrower sense.

(수계받은)

Here, we will focus on the _____. (후자)

The Buddha _____ many people. (조언하다)

Avoid _____ _____ from following the spiritual path.

(마음이 흐트러짐)

To have a group of _____ _____ named the Sangha. (도반)

This is half of the holy life, _____. (세존)

_____ _____ is actually the whole of the holy life.

(좋은 벗, 훌륭한 친구)

Develop and practice the _____ _____ _____. (팔정도)

Questions

1. The Sangha has two meanings. What are they?

2. The fourfold Buddhist community consists of what?

3. When were you ordained?

4. Please name some of your spiritual friends!

5. Is the Sangha important for Buddhist practice?

6. Does "World-Honored-One" refer to the Buddha?

7. Is "Right View" an element of the Noble Eightfold Path?

4 삼보

삼보는 모든 불교의 근본이다.

불교의 삼보는 불·법·승이다.

부처는 사람들에게 도를 처음으로 가르쳐준 '깨달으신 분'이다.

법은 불교의 가르침을 총괄하여 일컫는 말이다. 부처님은 깨달으신 후 깊은 고민에 빠졌다. 바로 자신이 아는 것을 전할 것인가 말 것인가였다. 하지만 자비심을 일으켜 부처님은 가르침을 전하기로 했다. 이 가르침들이 '법(다르마)'이라고 알려지게 되었다.

승가는 부처님의 가르침을 실천하는 수행자 집단을 의미한다. 승가는 불자들의 중심기관으로, 스님들은 계를 받은 후에 열심히 수행하여 재가자들이 해탈할 수 있도록 가르친다.

Unit 4 The Three Jewels

The Three Jewels are the foundation of all forms of Buddhism.

The Three Jewels of Buddhism are: the Buddha, the Dharma and the Sangha.

The Buddha is the Enlightened One who first showed others the path.

The Dharma is the collective term for the teachings of Buddhism.

The Buddha faced a great dilemma after his enlightenment — whether he should pass on his understanding or not. But out of compassion, he decided to pass on his teachings. These teachings came to be known as the Dharma.

The Sangha is the community of all Buddhists who practice the Buddha's teachings. The Sangha is the central institution of Buddhism, where monks and nuns, after taking vows, devote their lives to Buddhist practice and to teaching the laity to help them attain liberation.

Fill in the Blanks

The Three Jewels are the _____ of all forms of Buddhism. (근본)

The Three Jewels of Buddhism are: the _____ , the _____ and the

_____ . (불 · 법 · 승)

The Buddha is the _____ _____ . (깨달으신 분)

The Dharma is the _____ of Buddhism. (가르침)

Whether he should _____ _____ his understanding or not. (전하다)

But out of _____ he decided to pass on his teachings. (자비심)

The Sangha is the community of all Buddhists who _____ the Buddha's

teachings. (수행하다)

After _____ _____ , they devote their lives to Buddhist practice.

(계를 받다)

Teach the laity to help them attain _____ . (해탈)

Questions   1. What are the Three Jewels of Buddhism?

2. Is the Dharma a component of the Three Jewels of Buddhism?

3. Does the Dharma refer to the teachings of the Buddha?

4. Did the Buddha face a dilemma after his awakening?

5. Did the Buddha decide to pass on his understanding?

6. What motivated the Buddha to pass on his understanding?

7. When do Buddhist monks and nuns take vows?

5 삼귀의

불자가 된다는 것은 삼보에 귀의하는 것이다.

삼보는 불·법·승을 말한다.

삼보에 대한 귀의는 다음을 염송하며 한다.

부처님께 귀의합니다.

법에 귀의합니다.

승가에 귀의합니다.

우리가 칭찬을 하든 욕을 하든 보석의 본질과 덕성이 변하지 않는 것처럼 삼보의 수승함 역시 그러하다. 불자들은 삼보를 의지처로 삼아 고통에서 벗어나 참자성을 깨달을 수 있다.

Unit 5 **Refuge in the Three Jewels**

To become a Buddhist is to take refuge in the Three Jewels.

The Three Jewels are the Buddha, the Dharma and the Sangha.

One takes the three refuges by reciting these lines;

I take refuge in the Buddha.

I take refuge in the Dharma.

I take refuge in the Sangha.

Just as real jewels never change their essence and goodness, whether praised or blamed, so are the unsurpassed qualities of the Three Jewels. Buddhists can rely on the Three Jewels as their refuge in order to be free from suffering and awaken to the true nature of all things.

To become a Buddhist is to _____ _____ in the Three Jewels.

(귀의하다)

The _____ _____ are the Buddha, the Dharma and the Sangha.

(삼보)

I take refuge in the _____ . (불)

I take refuge in the _____ . (법)

I take refuge in the _____ . (승)

Jewels never change their _____ and goodness. (본질)

The _____ qualities of the Three Jewels. (위없는, 수승한)

Buddhists can _____ _____ the Three Jewels as their refuge.

(의지하다)

Questions   1. Do you take refuge in the Three Jewels at Buddhist ceremonies?

2. What are the Three Jewels?

3. Why are the Three Jewels called "Jewels"?

4. How do you feel when you are praised?

5. How do you feel when you are blamed?

6. Does the Buddha have unsurpassed qualities?

7. Did the Buddha attain unsurpassed enlightenment?

6 사대

우리가 이 몸에 머무는 동안 단단한 것은 지대이고, 습한 것은 수대이며, 따스한 것은 화대이고, 움직이는 것은 풍대이다.

– 팔리 경전에서

불교에서 모든 물질은 사대에 의해 형성된다.

사대는 지대, 수대, 화대, 풍대이다.

이는 고체성, 유동성, 열기, 운동성을 의미할 수 있다.

사대는 현상계를 이루는 네 가지 기본적 물질 요소이다.

우주 만물은 모두 사대로 구성되어 있다.

부처님은 사대가 고통의 원인이라고 하셨다.

부처님은 또한 사대가 공하다고 하셨다.

이는 모든 물질 현상은 실체가 없음을 의미한다.

변하지 않는 것은 없다.

우리가 세상의 참모습을 이해하지 못할 때 고통이 온다.

Unit 6 The Four Great Elements

While you are in your body, what is solid is of earth, what is moist is of water, what is warm is of fire, and what moves is of wind.

- From a Pali text

In Buddhism, all matter is formed by the four great elements.

They are earth, water, fire and wind.

They may represent solidity, fluidity, heat and motion.

They are the four basic material components of the phenomenal world.
All things in the universe consist of the four great elements.

The Buddha said that the four great elements cause suffering.

The Buddha also said that the four great elements are intrinsically empty.

This means that all material phenomena are without any real substance.

There is nothing that does not change.

When we fail to understand the true nature of the world, we suffer.

Fill in the Blanks

What is solid is of _____ . (지)

What is moist is of _____ . (수)

What is warm is of _____ . (화)

What moves is of _____ . (풍)

In Buddhism, all matter is formed by the _____ _____ _____ .

(사대)

All things in the universe _____ _____ the four great elements.

(구성되다)

The Buddha said that the four great elements cause _____ . (괴로움)

The Buddha also said that the four great elements are intrinsically _____ .

(공하다)

This means that all material phenomena are without any real _____ .

(실체)

Questions

1. What are the four great elements?

2. What quality does water represent?

3. Is all matter formed by the four great elements?

4. Did the Buddha say the four great elements cause suffering?

5. Do the four great elements have any substance?

6. Does the phenomenal world consist of the four great elements?

7. Is there anything that does not change in this world?

7 사성제

사성제는 불교 가르침의 정수를 이룬다.

사성제는 괴로움의 진리, 괴로움의 원인의 진리, 괴로움의 멸의 진리, 괴로움을 멸하는 길의 진리이다.

간단히 말해서, 괴로움이 있다 · 괴로움에는 원인이 있다 · 괴로움에는 끝이 있다 · 괴로움의 끝을 야기하는 원인이 있다는 것이다.

괴로움의 개념은 부정적 관점을 나타내지 않는다.

괴로움은 세상을 있는 그대로 대할 수 있도록 도와준다.

즐거움의 개념은 순간적이라고 인정되고 있다.

즐거움의 추구는 해소할 수 없는 갈증으로 귀착된다.

괴로움의 원인은 번뇌이다.

괴로움을 멸하기 위해 따라야 할 길은 팔정도이다.

 The Four Noble Truths

The Four Noble Truths comprise the essence of Buddha's teachings.

They are: the truth of suffering, the truth of the cause of suffering, the truth of the end of suffering, and the truth of the path that leads to the end of suffering.

In simpler words: suffering exists; it has a cause; it has an end; and it has a cause to bring about its end.

The notion of suffering does not represent a negative world view.

It helps us to deal with the world as it is.

The concept of pleasure is acknowledged as fleeting.

Pursuit of pleasure only results in an unquenchable thirst.

The causes of suffering are afflictions.

The path to follow for the cessation of suffering is the Noble Eightfold Path.

The Four Noble Truths comprise the _____ of Buddha's teachings.

(본질, 정수)

The truth of _____ . (괴로움)

The truth of the _____ of suffering. (원인)

The truth of the _____ of suffering. (끝)

The truth of the _____ that leads to the end of suffering. (길)

The notion of suffering does not represent a _____ world view. (부정적인)

The concept of pleasure is acknowledged as _____ . (순간적인)

_____ of pleasure only results in an unquenchable thirst. (추구)

The causes of suffering are _____ . (번뇌)

Questions

1. What are the Four Noble Truths?

2. Does suffering have a cause?

3. According to Buddhism, what is the cause of suffering?

4. Is there a path that leads to the end of suffering?

5. If you embrace suffering, does it help you deal with the world as it is?

6. Is pleasure permanent?

7. Have you ever experienced an unquenchable thirst?

팔정도

깨달음을 얻고자 하면 팔정도를 수행하라.

그리하면 기쁨과 평안, 지혜를 얻으리라.　　　　　　　　　– 부처님이 수바드라에게 남긴 유훈

팔정도는 불교의 근간이며 올바른 삶을 살아가는 지침이다. 부처님은 5비구에게 했던 최초의 설법에서 팔정도를 가르쳤고, 이후로도 45년간 계속하여 가르치셨다.

1. 정견: 사물을 있는 그대로 바르게 이해하기

2. 정사유: 바르게 생각하기

3. 정어: 정직하고 진실되게 말하기

4. 정업: 바르고 자비롭게 행동하기

5. 정명: 바른 방식으로 생계를 유지하기

6. 정정진: 바르고 꾸준하게 정진하기

7. 정념: 매 순간 깨어서 알아차리기

8. 정정: 마음을 바르게 안정시키기

Unit 8 The Noble Eightfold Path of Buddhism

If you want to be enlightened, practice the Noble Eightfold Path.
If you do so, you will achieve joy, peace and wisdom.

- The Buddha's Last Teaching to Subhadda

The Noble Eightfold Path is the foundation of Buddhism and provides the basic guidelines for virtuous living. The Buddha taught the Noble Eightfold Path in his first teachings to his five disciples and continuously taught it for the next 45 years.

1. Right View: To understand things correctly as they are.

2. Right Thought: To think in a right way.

3. Right Speech: To speak honestly and truthfully.

4. Right Action: To act in right and compassionate ways.

5. Right Livelihood: To make a living in the right way.

6. Right Effort: To make right and steady effort diligently.

7. Right Mindfulness: To be awake and mindful in every moment.

8. Right Concentration: To stabilize the mind correctly.

Fill in the Blanks

If you want to be enlightened, _____ the Noble Eightfold Path.

(실천하다, 수행하다)

The Noble Eightfold Path is the _____ of Buddhism. (근간)

The Buddha taught the Noble Eightfold Path in his first teachings to his

_____ _____ . (5비구)

_____ _____ : To understand things correctly as they are. (정견)

_____ _____ : To think in a right way. (정사유)

_____ _____ : To speak honestly and truthfully. (정어)

_____ _____ : To act in right and compassionate ways. (정업)

_____ _____ : To make a living in the right way. (정명)

_____ _____ : To make right and steady effort diligently. (정정진)

_____ _____ : To be awake and mindful in every moment. (정념)

_____ _____ : To stabilize the mind correctly. (정정)

Questions
1. Is the Noble Eightfold Path the path to enlightenment?
2. What are the basic guidelines for virtuous living?
3. Did the Buddha teach the Noble Eightfold Path to his three disciples?
4. Did the Buddha keep teaching the Noble Eightfold Path?
5. What is Right View?
6. What is Right Livelihood?
7. What is Right Mindfulness?

9 육바라밀

산스크리트어 '바라밀'은 '건너편 언덕으로 건너간다'를 의미한다.

육바라밀의 수행을 통해 우리는 윤회의 고해를 건너 행복과 깨달음(열반)의 언덕으로 건너갈 수 있다.

1. 보시바라밀: 보시는 집착과 기대가 전혀 없는 것이다. 보시에는 세 가지가 있다:
   재시(財施) · 법시(法施) · 무외시(無畏施).

2. 지계바라밀: 계율을 지키며 사는 것. 생각, 말, 행동이 덕스럽고 무해한 것.

3. 인욕바라밀: 삶의 어려움을 내적 평정심을 잃지 않고 직면하게 해주는 마음의 힘. 역경과 모욕을 인내로 앙심 없이 받아들이는 것.

4. 정진바라밀: 최상의 깨달음을 얻기 위하여 법과 다른 5바라밀을 부지런히 닦는 것.

5. 선정바라밀: 명상을 통해 우리가 하는 모든 일에 깨어 있고 그것을 알아차림으로써 마음을 안정시키는 것.

6. 지혜바라밀: 언어와 개념을 초월한 최상의 지혜.

Unit 9 The Six Paramitas (Perfections)

The Sanskrit word "paramita" means to "cross over to the other shore." Through the practice of these six paramitas, we cross over the sea of suffering (samsara) to the shore of happiness and enlightenment (Nirvana).

1. The Perfection of Generosity: Giving which is completely free from attachment and expectation. There are three forms of giving: material things, the Dharma, and courage.

2. The Perfection of Ethics: Living life observing the precepts; Being virtuous and harmless in one's thoughts, speech and actions.

3. The Perfection of Patience: The strength of mind that enables us to face the challenges of life without losing our inner tranquility. Embracing adversity and insults with patience free of resentment.

4. The Perfection of Joyous Effort: Diligently practicing the Dharma and the other five paramitas to pursue the supreme goal of enlightenment.

5. The Perfection of Concentration: Stabilizing the mind by practicing meditation, by being mindful and aware in everything we do.

6. The Perfection of Wisdom: The supreme wisdom beyond words and concepts.

Fill in the Blanks

_____ means to 'cross over to the other shore.' (바라밀)

Through the practice of these _____ _____, we cross over the sea of suffering (samsara). (육바라밀)

The Perfection of _____: Giving which is completely free from attachment and expectation. (보시)

The Perfection of _____: Living life observing the precepts. (지계, 윤리)

The Perfection of _____: The strength of mind that enables us to face the challenges of life without losing our inner tranquility. (인욕, 인내)

The Perfection of _____ _____: Diligently practicing the Dharma and the other five paramitas. (정진, 즐거운 정진)

The Perfection of _____: Stabilizing the mind by practicing meditation.

(선정)

The Perfection of _____: The supreme wisdom beyond words and concepts. (지혜)

Questions

1. Does "paramita" mean to "cross over to the other shore?"
2. What do "this shore" and the "other shore" mean?
3. What are the three forms of giving?
4. If you live observing the precepts, which perfection are you practicing?
5. When you are virtuous in your thoughts, are you practicing the Perfection of Ethics?
6. What is the way of practicing the Perfection of Concentration?
7. What are the six paramitas?

10 연기

부처님은 당신의 깨달음을 '연기의 법칙'이라는 개념으로 요약하셨다.

연기의 법칙은 다음을 가르친다.

– 만물은 복잡한 조건들의 그물망에 의해 생겨나고 유지된다.

– 다른 것으로부터 완전히 독립하여 존재하는 것은 없다.

– 만물은 그것을 유지하는 조건들이 멸하게 되면 소멸한다.

– 존재는 끝없는 변화의 과정이다.

12연기는 윤회적 삶에서 하나가 또 하나를 생성하게 하는 인연을 서술한다.

1. 무명(無明) 2. 행(行) 3. 식(識) 4. 명색(名色) 5. 육입(六入) 6. 촉(觸) 7. 수(受)

8. 애(愛) 9. 취(取) 10. 유(有) 11. 생(生) 12. 노사(老死).

Unit 10 Dependent Origination

The Buddha summarized his enlightenment in the concept of "Principle of Dependent Origination."

This principle teaches;

- Everything comes into being and is maintained by a complex web of conditions.

- Nothing exists completely independent of anything else.

- Everything ceases when the conditions that maintain it cease.

- Existence is a ceaseless process of flux.

The twelve links of dependent origination describe a causal connection between the subsequent conditions of cyclic existence, each one giving rise to the next:

1. ignorance 2. mental formations 3. consciousness 4. name and form
5. the six sense gates (eyes, ears, nose, tongue, body and mind)
6. contact 7. feeling 8. craving 9. clinging 10. becoming 11. birth
12. ageing and death.

Fill in the Blanks

The Buddha _____ his enlightenment in the concept of "Principle of
Dependent Origination." (요약하다)

Nothing exists completely _____ _____ anything else. (독립하여)

Everything ceases when the _____ that maintain it cease. (조건들)

Consciousness arises depending on _____ _____ . (행)

Feeling arises depending on _____ . (촉)

Clinging arises depending on _____ . (갈애)

Birth arises depending on _____ . (유)

Questions

1. Is there anything that exists completely independent of anything
   else?
2. What arises depending on ignorance?
3. What arises depending on consciousness?
4. What arises depending on the six sense gates?
5. What arises depending on feeling?
6. What arises depending on clinging?
7. What arises depending on birth?

11 십이처

무안이비설신의　無眼耳鼻舌身意

무색성향미촉법　無色聲香味觸法　　　　　　　　　　　– 《반야심경》

여기서 '안(眼), 이(耳), 비(鼻), 설(舌), 신(身), 의(意)'를 육근(六根)이라 하고, '색(色), 성(聲), 향(香), 미(味), 촉(觸), 법(法)'을 육경(六境)이라 한다. 육근과 육경을 합쳐 십이처(十二處)라고 한다. '안(眼)과 색(色)', '이(耳)와 성(聲)' 등이 근거가 되어 마음 작용이 일어나 세상이 우리 에게 드러나는 것이다. 이는 인간을 중심으로 한 관점으로서 '나'라고 하는 주관적 존재와, 내 외부에 나타나는 객관세계를 합쳐 일체(一切)라고 하는 것이다.

대승불교의 관점에서 생각해 보면, 십이처는 항상하지도 않고, 고정된 실체가 있는 것도 아 니다. 그러므로 스스로의 자성(自性)이 없으며 공하다고 하는 것이다. 그래서 '무안이비설 신의 무색성향미촉법'이라는 말로써 육근과 육경을 부정한다. 십이처를 부정함으로써 공 (空)의 참모습을 드러내고 있는 것이다.

– 법상 스님의 《반야심경》 강해 (http://moktaksori.net/)

Unit 11　The Twelve Sense Fields

Therefore, in emptiness there are no eyes, ears, nose, tongue, body or mind; no sights, sounds, smells, tastes, objects of touch or dharmas.

- From the *Heart Sutra*

Here, the "eyes, ears, nose, tongue, body or mind" are called the "six sense faculties" and "sights, sounds, smells, tastes, objects of touch or dharmas" are called the six objects of the senses. The six sense faculties and the six objects of the senses compose the "twelve sense fields." For example, mind arises based on the encounter of "eyes and sights" or "ears and sounds," through which we perceive the world. This is a people-oriented perspective. There is a subjective self called "I" and the objective world outside of me: The combination of these two is called "all things."

From the perspective of Mahayana Buddhism, the twelve sense fields are not permanent and do not have fixed substance. Therefore, they are said to be void of self-nature and empty. The above passage cited from the *Heart Sutra* denies the six sense faculties and their corresponding objects. By denying the twelve sense fields, the true nature of emptiness is revealed.

- Lecture on the *Heart Sutra* by Ven. Beopsang

Fill in the Blanks

The "eyes, ears, nose, tongue, body or mind" are called the _____ _____ _____. (육근)

The "sights, sounds, smells, tastes, objects of touch or dharmas" are called the _____ _____ of the senses. (육경)

The six sense faculties and the six objects of the senses compose the "_____ _____ _____." (십이처)

Mind _____ based on the encounter of "eyes and sights." (일어난다)

From the _____ of Mahayana Buddhism. (관점)

The twelve sense fields do not have _____ _____. (고정된 실체)

Therefore, they are said to be _____ _____ self-nature and empty. (없다, 공하다)

The above passage _____ from the *Heart Sutra*. (인용한)

The true nature of emptiness is _____. (드러나다)

Questions

1. What are the six sense faculties?
2. What are the six objects of the senses?
3. What are the twelve sense fields?
4. Does the mind arise when the eyes encounter sights?
5. Do the twelve sense fields have fixed substance?
6. Does the *Heart Sutra* affirm the twelve sense fields?
7. Does the *Heart Sutra* reveal the true nature of emptiness?

12 삼법인

모든 불교의 가르침은 삼법인을 가지고 있다. 삼법인이 없다면 그 가르침은 불교의 가르침이라 할 수 없다.

1. 제행무상(諸行無常): 인연 따라 모인 모든 것은 항상하지 않는다. 우리가 사랑하는 사람들과 물건들은 영원히 우리 곁에 있지는 않을 것이다. 그래서 그들이 더욱 소중하다. 또한 불행을 비롯한 모든 것은 변한다는 사실을 안다면 불쾌한 상황도 더 나아지리라는 희망을 품어볼 수 있다.

2. 제법무아(諸法無我): 독립되고 고정된 자성을 가진 것은 하나도 없다. 다만 사대가 일시적으로 모인 것이다. 인연이 다하면 일시적으로 모인 것들은 흩어진다.

3. 열반적정(涅槃寂靜): '나와 너' '생과 사' '득과 실'이라는 이원적 개념이 사라질 때 우리 마음은 맑고 고요하게 된다. 그때 우리는 진정한 행복이 물질적 삶, 자기중심적 삶에 있지 않다는 것을 알게 된다.

Unit 12 The Three Dharma Seals

Every Buddhist teaching bears the Three Dharma Seals. Without all three seals the teaching is not a Buddhist teaching.

1. Impermanence: All composite things are impermanent. People and the things we love will not be with us forever. We will thus value them even more. Also, knowing that everything changes, including unhappiness, gives us the hope that unpleasant circumstances may improve for the better.

2. Non-self: Nothing has an independent, fixed self. It is just a temporary aggregate of the four great elements. When the causes and conditions cease, the temporary aggregates will be dispersed.

3. Nirvana: When the dual ideas of self and other, birth and death, gain and loss are extinguished, one becomes calm and clear. Then we will understand that genuine happiness is not to be found in a materialistic, self-centered existence.

Every Buddhist teaching bears the _____ _____ _____ .

(삼법인)

All _____ things are impermanent. (조합된)

It gives us the hope that unpleasant circumstances may _____ for the better. (개선되다, 나아지다)

Nothing has an independent, _____ _____ . (고정된 자아)

It is just a temporary _____ of the four great elements. (집합)

When the _____ and _____ cease. (인연)

When the _____ _____ are extinguished. (이원적 생각, 이분법)

Genuine happiness is not to be found in a materialistic, _____ existence.

(자기중심적인)

Questions
1. What does every Buddhist teaching bear?
2. Are all conditioned things permanent?
3. Which Buddhist principle lets us know that even unpleasant circumstances will change?
4. Do you have an independent, fixed self?
5. Are your temporary aggregates composed of the four great elements?
6. When are the temporary aggregates dispersed?
7. What is duality or a dual idea?

135

⑬ 중도

이 양 극단을 피함으로써 여래는 중도를 깨달았다. 중도는 예지력을 주고, 지식을 주고, 고요한 마음, 통찰력, 깨달음, 열반으로 이끌어준다. 여래가 깨달은 중도란 무엇인가? 그것은 바로 팔정도이다.

– 《전법륜경》

중도는 존재의 양극단을 초월하는 직관적 지식을 일컫는다. 중도는 직선의 양극단 중간 지점을 의미하지 않는다. 중도는 역동적인 가르침이다. 부처님은 강가에 앉아 지나가는 배에서 나는 류트 소리를 들으며 중도의 의미를 깨달았다. 조화로운 소리를 내려면 류트 줄이 너무 세게 조여도 너무 느슨하게 풀려도 안 된다는 것을 이해하셨던 것이다.

실재는 궁극적으로 정의할 수 없다. 그 무엇도 '이것' 또는 '저것'이라 확신할 수 없다. 삶의 모든 것은 늘상 변화하고 있는 다른 것들에 연하여 생겨난다. 이는 그 무엇도 완전히 독립하여 존재하지 않음을 의미한다. 이렇게 연기(緣起)를 이해하고 그 이해를 바탕으로 팔정도를 실천하면 중도를 수행하는 것이다.

Unit 13 The Middle Way

Avoiding both these extremes, the Tathagata has realized the Middle Way; it gives vision, gives knowledge, and leads to calm, to insight, to enlightenment and to Nirvana. And what is that Middle Way realized by the Tathagata? It is the Noble Eightfold Path, and nothing else.

- *Dhammacakkappavattana Sutta* (SN 56.11)

The Middle Way refers to the direct knowledge that transcends the polarized duality of existence. The Middle Way does not mean a mid-point on a straight line joining two extremes. The Middle Way is a dynamic teaching. The Buddha realized the meaning of the Middle Way when he sat by a river and heard a lute player in a passing boat. He understood that the lute string must be tuned neither too tight nor too loose to produce a harmonious sound.

Reality is ultimately indefinable. Nothing can be pinned down to be either "this" or "that." Everything in life arises dependent on other things, which keep changing. This means that nothing is completely independent. When we understand the principle of dependent origination in this way and practice the Noble Eightfold Path based on that understanding, we can practice the Middle Way.

Fill in the Blanks

Avoiding both these extremes, the Tathagata has realized the _____ _____ . (중도)

The Middle Way transcends the polarized _____ of existence.

(이원성, 이분법)

The Middle Way is a _____ teaching. (역동적인)

When he sat by a river and heard a lute player in a _____ _____ .

(지나가는 배)

The lute string must be tuned neither too _____ nor too _____ .

(세게, 느슨하게)

Reality is _____ indefinable. (궁극적으로)

Everything in life arises _____ _____ other things.

(의지하여, 연하여)

This means that nothing is completely _____ . (독립적)

Questions

1. Did the Buddha realize the Middle Way by avoiding both extremes?
2. What is the Middle Way realized by the Buddha?
3. Does the Middle Way mean a mid-point on a straight line joining two extremes?
4. Can you define reality with words?
5. Does everything arise dependent on something else?

137

삼학

불자는 부처가 되기 위해 수학하는 사람이다. 삼학은 계 · 정 · 혜로 구성된다.

계학은 무해의 덕을 닦는 수행으로, 이 덕을 자신의 삶과 모든 인간관계로 넓혀 수행하는 것이다. 이는 자신의 생각, 말, 행동이 남들과 자신의 삶 전반에 미치는 결과를 숙고하는 것이다.

정학은 마음을 고요하고 맑게 하는 것이다. 이 공부는 마음을 윤택하고, 절도있고, 맑고, 고요하고, 집중하고, 비게 하는 데 목적이 있다.

혜학은 정학이 이룬 결과다. 명상은 우리 마음을 고요하고 지혜롭게 해준다. 마음이 고요하면 우리는 사물을 좀더 명료하게 보게 되고, 평소에는 명확하지 않던 심오한 진리를 깨닫게 된다. 따라서 지혜는 명상과 연계하여 생겨난다.

Unit 14 The Three Trainings of Buddhism

A Buddhist is a person engaged in training to become a buddha. The three trainings consist of ethics, meditation and wisdom.

Training in ethics cultivates the virtue of non-harming and to practice and extend this virtue into every aspect of one's life and into all one's relationships. This means reflecting upon the consequences of one's every thought, word and deed on others and the general atmosphere surrounding one's life.

Training in meditation helps one achieve calm and clarity of mind. This training aims to make the mind supple, disciplined, clear, tranquil, focused and empty.

Training in wisdom results from the training in meditation. Meditation tends to make our minds still and insightful. When the mind is, still we tend to see things more clearly and often realize deeper truths which are not clear during normal thinking. Thus, wisdom comes in connection with meditation.

A Buddhist is a person engaged in _____ to become a buddha.

(수학하다, 닦다)

The three trainings consist of ethics, _____ and wisdom. (명상, 정)

Training in ethics cultivates the virtue of _____ . (무해)

This means reflecting upon the _____ of one's every thought, word and deed. (결과, 영향)

Training in meditation helps one achieve _____ and _____ of mind. (적적성성, 고요하고 맑음)

Training in wisdom _____ _____ the training in meditation.

(~로부터 나오다)

Meditation tends to make our minds still and _____ . (통찰력 있는)

When the mind is still, we tend to see things more _____ . (맑게, 명료하게)

1. Do Buddhists train themselves to become buddhas?

2. What are the three trainings of Buddhism?

3. What does training in ethics cultivate?

4. Do Buddhists need to be discreet in their thoughts, words, and deeds?

5. What does training in meditation achieve?

6. Does meditation facilitate a calm and clear mind?

7. Does wisdom come in connection with meditation?

15 오계

이것은 간단해 보이지만 쉽지가 않다. 세 살배기도 알지만 80세 노인도 일상생활에서 이를 실제로 실천하기는 어렵다.

오계는 승가, 재가를 막론하고 모두가 더불어 행복한 삶을 살기 위해 지켜야 한다. 계를 지킴으로써 도덕성도 기를 뿐만 아니라 주변 생명들에게도 최고의 봉사를 하게 된다. 다음은 모든 사람들이 실천하고 준수해야 할 기본적인 계이다.

1. 살생하지 말라[不殺生]　　　　2. 도둑질하지 말라[不偸盜]

3. 음행을 하지 말라[不邪淫]　　　　4. 거짓말을 하지 말라[不妄語]

5. 술을 마시지 말라[不飮酒]

Unit 15 Leading a Buddhist Life and the Five Precepts

Not to do any evil

To cultivate good

To purify one's mind

This is the teaching of the Buddha.　　　- *Dhammapada*

It is simple but not easy. When a child is three years old, he knows it. However, when he is over 80 years old, he cannot really practice it in his daily life.

The five precepts should be observed by all Buddhists, monastic or lay, in order to lead a happy life. By observing the precepts, not only do you cultivate moral strength, but you also perform the highest service to your fellow beings. Following are the basic precepts that all people should practice and abide by.

1. Do not kill   2. Do not steal

3. Do not indulge in sexual misconduct

4. Do not make false speech   5. Do not take intoxicants

Fill in the Blanks

An 80-year-old man cannot practice it in his _____ _____ .

(일상생활)

The five precepts should be _____ by all Buddhists. (지키다)

By observing the precepts, you _____ moral strength. (닦다, 배양하다)

The basic precepts that all people should practice and _____ _____ .

(준수하다)

1. Do not _____ . (살생하다)

2. Do not _____ . (훔치다)

3. Do not indulge in _____ _____ . (부적절한 성행위)

4. Do not make _____ _____ . (거짓말)

5. Do not take _____ . (술, 취하게 하는 것)

Questions

1. What are the five precepts?

2. Are the five precepts only observed by monks and nuns?

3. Why do we need to observe the five precepts?

4. Do you receive the five precepts via special ceremonies?

5. Can you drink alcohol while observing the five precepts?

16 업

우리의 삶은 마음에 의해 형성된다. 우리가 생각하는 것이 바로 우리가 되는 것이다.
수레바퀴가 그것을 끄는 소를 따라가듯 악한 생각에는 고통이 따른다.　　　　－《법구경》

불교는 업의 법칙 때문에 변화가 가능하다고 말한다. '업'은 '행동'을 의미한다. 업의 법칙은 행동에는 과보가 따른다고 말한다. 즉 긍정적 행동에는 긍정적 과보가, 부정적 행동에는 부정적 과보가 따르는 것이다.

주변을 둘러보면 이 법칙의 증거가 보인다. 하나의 씨앗이 변하여 꽃이 된다. 우리가 운동을 하면 몸이 튼튼해진다. 불교는 우리 마음도 이와 같이 할 수 있다고 말한다. 지금 어떻게 행동할 것인지를 선택함으로써 미래의 행복을 창출할 수 있는 것이다.

우리가 행동하고 생각하고 말하는 모든 것은 우리 자신과 주변 세상에 영향을 미친다. 변화는 어떤 방식으로든 우리에게 일어나겠지만 어떻게 행동할 것인지 우리가 하는 선택에 따라 우리는 자신과 주변 세상을 더 낫게 변화시킬 수 있다.

Unit 16　Karma, the Law of Cause and Effect

Our life is shaped by our mind: we become what we think. Suffering follows an evil thought as the wheels of a cart follow the oxen that draw it.

- Dhammapada

Buddhism says that change is possible because of the Law of Karma. The word "karma" means "action." The Law of Karma states that actions have consequences: positive actions have positive consequences; negative actions have negative consequences.

We can see evidence of this all around us: a seed changes to become a flower; if we exercise, we become fitter. Buddhism says that we can even do the same with our hearts and minds. By choosing how we act now, we create our future happiness.

Everything we do, think or say has an effect on the world around us and on us. Change will happen to us anyway, but through the choices we make about how to behave, we can change ourselves, and the world around us, for the better.

- Adapted from the website (www.clear-vision.org)

Fill in the Blanks

Our life is shaped by our _____ . (마음)

We become what we _____ . (생각하다)

Suffering follows an _____ _____ . (악한 생각)

The word karma means "_____." (행동)

The Law of Karma states that actions have _____ . (과보)

Positive actions have _____ _____ . (선한 과보)

Negative actions have _____ _____ . (악한 과보)

We can see _____ of this all around us. (증거)

A seed _____ to become a flower. (변하다)

If we exercise we become _____ . (더 건강한, 컨디션이 더 좋은)

By _____ how we act now, we create our future happiness. (선택하다)

We can change ourselves for the _____ . (더 낫게)

Questions

1. What does karma mean?

2. Does the Law of Karma follow the law of cause and effect?

3. Do positive actions bring about positive consequences?

4. Does the Law of Karma suggest fatalism?

5. Can we create our future happiness by choosing how we act now?

17 육도윤회

중생은 즐거움을 탐하고 고통을 혐오한다. 이런 마음자세의 지배를 받아 그들은 윤회를 반복하고 사후 다음 생의 인연을 스스로 만들어낸다. 본인의 의지와 상관없이 윤회계의 탄생은 계속된다. 불자들은 이런 인연(원인과 조건)을 절멸함으로써 윤회를 끊어버리고자 한다. 불교는 우주의 모든 것으로부터 독립한 '나'라는 것은 궁극적으로 없다고 말한다. 계속 이어지는 삶으로의 탄생은 업에 의해 좌우되는 '연기'의 과정의 연속으로 이해되어야 한다.

탄생은 여섯 가지 영역인 육도 중 하나에서 이루어진다.

1. 지옥도(地獄道)   2. 아귀도(餓鬼道)   3. 축생도(畜生道)
4. 아수라도(阿修羅道)   5. 인도(人道)   6. 천도(天道)

 ## Samsara, The Cycle of Conditioned Existence and Suffering

Sentient beings crave pleasure and hate pain. In being controlled by these attitudes, they perpetuate the cycle of conditioned existence and suffering, and produce the causes and conditions of the next rebirth after death. Each rebirth repeats this process in an involuntary cycle. Buddhists strive to end this cycle by eradicating the causes and conditions.

According to Buddhism there ultimately is no such thing as a self independent from the rest of the universe. Rebirth in subsequent existences must be understood as the continuation of a dynamic, ever-changing process of "dependent arising" determined by one's karma.

Each rebirth takes place within one of the six realms.

1. Hell   2. Hungry ghosts

3. Animals   4. Asuras: demons

5. Human beings   6. Heavenly beings: Devas

Sentient beings _____ pleasure and hate pain. (탐닉하다)

Sentient beings _____ the cycle of conditioned existence. (끊임없이 계속 한다)

Buddhists strive to end this cycle by eradicating the _____ and _____ . (인연, 원인과 조건)

There is no such thing as a self _____ _____ the rest of the universe. (독립하여 존재하는)

Each rebirth takes place within one of the six _____ . (영역, 도)

1. _____ (지옥)

2. _____ _____ (아귀)

3. _____ (축생)

4. _____ (아수라)

5. _____ (인간)

6. _____ _____ (천인)

Questions

1. What does samsara mean?

2. How many realms do sentient beings wander in samsara?

3. Can you sever the cycle of birth and death?

4. Is continued rebirth propelled by karma?

5. Is the cycle of conditioned existence a result of dependent origination?

18 상수제자

"내가 사리불과 목건련을 거느렸듯이 모든 과거불도 다 한 쌍의 상수제자를 거느렸으며 모든 미래불도 한 쌍의 제자를 거느릴 것이다." — 《상응부》(47 : 14)

승단체제 안에서 상수제자의 기본적 역할은 세 가지라고 할 수 있다. 불법이 굳건히 뿌리내려 인간과 천상의 많은 존재에게 정신적 변화를 가져올 수 있도록 세존을 도와 드리는 것이 그 첫째이다. 둘째는 다른 비구들의 수행을 지도하면서 본받을 만한 모범이 되는 일이다. 셋째는 승가의 운영을 돕는 일이다. 특히 세존께서 독거에 드시거나 긴요한 일로 홀로 길을 떠나시면 승가를 돌보아야 한다.

사리불과 목건련이 수계를 받을 때 부처님은 이들이 상수제자라고 말씀했다. 두 사람은 곧 아라한이 되었다. 부처님은 사리불이 완벽한 제자이며, 지혜에서 부처님 다음이라 하셨다. 사리불은 부처님의 승낙 하에 자주 대중에게 설법을 했다. 사리불 다음으로 지혜가 높았던 목건련은 신통제일이었다.

Unit 18 Chief Disciples

As I have Sariputra and Maudgalyayana, all buddhas of the past had two chief disciples and all buddhas of the future will too.

- *Samyukta Nikaya* (SN 47 : 14)

In the monastic system of the Sangha, chief disciples basically perform three functions. First, they help the Buddha to make the Buddha-dharma take firm root, thereby bringing about spiritual transformation for humans and heavenly beings. Second, they give guidance to the practice of other monks and become model practitioners themselves. Third, they help run the operation of the Sangha. Especially, when the Buddha went on a solo retreat or made a trip to a distant place, they needed to take care of the Sangha.

On the day Sariputra and Maudgalyayana were ordained, the Buddha declared them to be his two chief disciples. Both soon became arhats.

The Buddha declared Sariputra to be a perfect disciple and second only to himself in wisdom. Sariputra frequently taught with the Buddha's approval. Second in wisdom only to Sariputra, Maudgalyayana was pre-eminent in miraculous powers.

Fill in the Blanks

All buddhas of the past had two _____ _____. (상수제자)

Chief disciples basically perform three _____. (기능, 역할)

They help the Buddha to make the Buddha-dharma take _____ _____. (굳게 뿌리내리게 하다)

They bring about spiritual _____ for humans. (변화)

They _____ _____ to the practice of other monks. (지도하다)

They become _____ practitioners themselves. (모범)

When the Buddha went into a _____ _____. (독거 안거)

They needed to take _____ of the Sangha. (돌보다)

When Sariputra and Maudgalyayana were _____, (수계받다)

The Buddha _____ them to be his two chief disciples. (선언하다)

Both soon became _____. (아라한)

Sariputra was foremost in _____. (지혜)

Maudgalyayana was eminent in _____ _____. (신통력)

Questions

1. Who were the two chief disciples of the Buddha?
2. Did Sariputra give guidance to other monks?
3. Did Maudgalyayana take care of the Sangha in the absence of the Buddha?
4. Did Sariputra and Maudgalyayana become arhats?
5. What was Sariputra foremost in?
6. What was Maudgalyayana foremost in?
7. How can you become a model practitioner in the Sangha?

19 사부대중

나는 우리 법맥의 모든 사찰이 비구, 비구니, 우바새, 우바이의 사부대중으로 이루어지기를 바라며, 사찰에 사는 재가자들은 승가와 재가 사회를 이어주는 다리가 되기를 바란다.

– 틱낫한

사부대중은 다음과 같이 구성된다: 비구 , 비구니, 우바새, 우바이.

사부대중 내의 자비로운 화합과 뒷받침은 중요하다. 부처님은 스님들이 재가자의 정신적 욕구를 소홀히 해서도 안 되며 또한 재가자와 지나치게 얽혀도 안 된다고 말씀하셨다. 승가가 재가로부터 너무 멀어지게 되면 재가자가 불법을 배우고 수행하는 데 지장이 올 것이며 이것이 계속되면 승가의 몰락이 올 것이다. 반면 재가가 승가를 멀리한다면 그 역시 완전한 사부대중을 이루었다고 볼 수 없는 것이다.

Unit 19 The Fourfold Community

I want all our monasteries to have a fourfold Sangha composed of monks, nuns, laymen, and laywomen, and for the laypeople living there to be a bridge between the monastic community and the laypeople society.

- Thich Nhat Hanh

The fourfold Sangha, or fourfold community, consists of:
Bhikshus (bhikkhus) - monks, Bhikshunis (bhikkhunis) - nuns
Upasakas - laymen, Upasikas - laywomen
Compassionate harmony and support within the fourfold Sangha is important. It was advised by the Buddha to neither neglect the spiritual needs of the lay people nor become inextricably intertwined with them. The sangha, if it became isolated from the laity, would lead to a decrease in the learning and practice of the Buddha-Dharma by the laity, and over time, result in the demise of the Sangha. If the laity isolates itself from the Sangha, it too cannot claim to be a complete fourfold community.

The _____ _____ or fourfold community consists of: (사부대중)

    Bhikshus (bhikkhus) - _____ (비구)

    Bhikshunis (bhikkhunis) - _____ (비구니)

    Upasakas - _____ (재가남성, 우바새)

    Upasikas - _____ (재가여성, 우바이)

Compassionate _____ within the fourfold Sangha is important. (화합)

Do not _____ the spiritual needs of the lay people. (소홀히 하다)

Do not become inextricably _____ with them. (뒤얽히다)

If the sangha became _____ _____ the laity. (격리되다, 소원해지다)

It would lead to the _____ of the Sangha. (몰락)

1. What does the fourfold Sangha consist of?

2. Is harmony of the fourfold Sangha important?

3. Do Bhikshus refer to Buddhist nuns?

4. Do Upasikas refer to laymen?

5. Should the monastic Sangha neglect the spiritual needs of the laity?

6. What would happen if the Sangha isolates itself from the laity?

20 수계

불도에 헌신하는 삶은 모든 사람이 다 할 수 있는 것은 아니다. 스님이 되기로 선택하는 것은 결코 쉽지 않은 삶을 살겠다는 것을 의미한다. 거기에는 고된 공부, 불도에서 이탈하지 않으려는 분투가 수반되며 매우 외로운 길이기도 하다. 그럼에도 불구하고 깨달음에 삶을 바치려는 사람들이 있다. 이들은 수계를 받고 스님으로서의 삶을 살아간다.

대승의 전통에서 비구계나 비구니계를 받겠다는 결정은 불도에 평생 헌신하겠다는 의지를 표명하는 것이다. 물론 후에 어떤 이유에서든 잘못된 결정을 내렸다고 생각되면 계를 반납할 수는 있다.

부처님 당시 초기의 승가에서는 부처님의 제자가 되고 싶은 사람은 단지 "오라, 비구여"라는 부처님의 말씀으로 스님이 될 수 있었지만 이후 좀더 격식을 갖춘 의식이 정립되었다.

한국에서 스님이 되고자 하는 지원자는 먼저 행자가 된다. 6~12개월 후 행자는 수계를 받고 사미·사미니가 된다. 사미·사미니가 4년제 교육을 마치면 구족계를 받을 자격이 주어진다.

Unit 20 Ordination

A life dedicated to the Buddhist path is not for everyone. To choose to be a monk or nun means to adopt a life that is not easy at all; it can involve a lot of hard work, a struggle to stay on the spiritual path, and it can be quite lonely. Still some people want to dedicate themselves to the attainment of Enlightenment. They receive ordination and take up the spiritual life of a monk or nun.

In Mahayana tradition, when a person decides to take the vows of a fully ordained Bhikshu or Bhikshuni, they are making a lifetime commitment to the Buddhist path. Of course, if later they decide for whatever reason, that they have made the wrong decision, they can always revoke their vows.

In the early days of the Buddha's Sangha, those who wanted to follow him were admitted simply with the words "Come, monk!" (Ehi bhikkhu), but a more formal ceremony was soon established.

In Korea an aspirant first becomes a postulant. After six to twelve months, a postulant can take vows and become a novice (Sanskrit: sramanera, sramanerika). When novices complete a training course of usually four years, they are eligible for full ordination.

- Adapted from the website (www.dharmafellowship.org)

Fill in the Blanks

A life _____ _____ the Buddhist path is not for everyone. (헌신하다)

It means to _____ a life that is not easy at all. (채택하다)

It can involve a struggle to _____ _____ the spiritual path.

(머물다)

Some people want to _____ enlightenment. (얻다)

They take up the _____ _____ of a monk or nun. (수도생활)

They are making a _____ _____ to the Buddhist path.

(평생의 약속)

They can always _____ their vows. (반환하다)

In Korea an aspirant first becomes a _____ . (행자)

After six to twelve months, a postulant can become a _____ . (사미)

When novices complete a training course of usually four years, they are eligible

for _____ _____ . (구족계)

Questions

1. Is a life dedicated to the Buddhist path easy?
2. What influenced you most when you chose to become a monk or nun?
3. Does it take a lot of hard work to stay on the spiritual path?
4. When did you receive ordination?
5. Is it a lifetime commitment to receive full ordination?
6. If you aspire to become a monastic in Korea, what do you do first?
7. How long do you need to be trained as a postulant before being eligible to become a novice?

21 상좌부불교

상좌부불교는 현존하는 가장 오래된 불교 종파이다. 상좌부는 비교적 보수적이고 일반적으로 초기불교에 가깝다고 할 수 있다. 상좌부는 동남아시아에서 주류를 이루고 그런 까닭에 '남방불교'라 부르기도 한다. 전세계에 약 1억 명의 신자가 있다. 교리는 주로 팔리 삼장에 근거한다. 상좌부에서는 예불을 거의 또는 전혀 중시하지 않고 명상을 통한 정신적 발전을 중시한다.

상좌부는 비판적 분석과 개인적 체험에서 얻는 통찰력을 강조한다. 상좌부는 개인의 깨달음을 강조하여 아라한이 되는 것을 이상으로 삼는다. 아라한은 깨달음을 얻고 생사의 고리에서 해탈한 사람이다. 상좌부의 무아는 대승불교의 무아와는 좀 다르다. 상좌부에게 무아는 개인의 자아가 굴레이며 망상이라는 의미이다. 이런 망상에서 벗어나고 나면 개인은 열반의 축복을 즐길 수 있다.

Unit 21 Theravada Buddhism

Theravada (the Teaching of the Elders) is the oldest surviving Buddhist school. It is relatively conservative, and generally closest to early Buddhism. Theravada is the dominant form of Buddhism in Southeast Asia, and for this reason, it is sometimes called the "Southern School." It claims about 100 million adherents worldwide. Its doctrines are based on the Pali Tipitaka. There is little or no worship in Theravada, and emphasis is on mental development through meditation.

Theravada emphasizes insight gained through critical analysis and personal experience. Theravada values individual enlightenment; the ideal is to become an arhat. An arhat is a person who has realized enlightenment and freed himself from the cycle of birth and death. Theravada's doctrine of anatman (non-self) differs from that of Mahayana: For Theravada, it means that an individual's ego is a fetter and a delusion. Once freed of this delusion, the individual may enjoy the bliss of Nirvana.

- Adapted from the website (http://buddhism.about.com)

Fill in the Blanks

Theravada is the oldest _____ Buddhist school. (살아남은)

It is generally closest to _____ _____. (초기불교)

Theravada is sometimes called the "_____ School." (남방)

Its doctrines are based on the _____ _____. (팔리 삼장)

Theravada's ideal is to become an _____. (아라한)

An arhat is a person who has realized _____. (깨달음)

An arhat has _____ himself from the cycle of birth and death.

(벗어나다, 자유롭다)

Once freed of this _____, the individual may enjoy the bliss of Nirvana.

(망상)

Questions

1. What is the oldest surviving Buddhist school?

2. Is Theravada Buddhism close to early Buddhism?

3. Where can you find Theravada Buddhism?

4. How many followers does Theravada Buddhism have?

5. Is the Pali Tipitaka the sacred scriptures of Theravada Buddhism?

6. What is the ideal that Theravada Buddhists pursue?

7. Is an arhat free from the cycle of birth and death?

22 대승불교

대승불교는 서기 1세기에 불교에 대한 좀더 자유롭고 접근 가능한 해석을 하며 출현하였다. '더 큰 수레'로써 대승은 스님과 고행자뿐 아니라 모든 계층의 사람들에게 열려 있는 불도 이다.

대승불교는 한국, 중국, 일본, 티베트, 몽골 등 북아시아와 극동아시아에서 주류를 이루며 따라서 '북방불교'라 부르기도 한다. 대승불자들은 팔리 삼장을 성전으로 받아들이지만 동시에 후대에 저술된 경전과 문헌들도 수용하고 있다.

상좌부가 개인적 깨달음을 중시한다면 대승은 모든 중생의 깨달음을 중시한다. 상좌부의 이상이 아라한이 되는 것이라면 대승의 이상은 보살이 되어 모든 중생을 생사윤회에서 구제하려고 한다. 보살이 모든 중생이 함께 깨달음을 얻도록 하려는 것은 자비심의 발로이기도 하지만 또한 우리가 서로에게서 분리될 수 없기 때문이다. 대승불자들은 깨달음을 한 생에 이룰 수 있고 또한 재가자도 그리할 수 있다고 말한다.

Unit 22 Mahayana Buddhism

Mahayana Buddhism emerged in the first century CE as a more liberal, accessible interpretation of Buddhism. As the "Greater Vehicle" (literally, the "Greater Ox-Cart"), Mahayana is a path available to people from all walks of life - not just monks and ascetics. Mahayana Buddhism is the predominant form of Buddhism in northern Asia and the Far East, including Korea, China, Japan, Tibet and Mongolia, and is thus sometimes known as Northern Buddhism. Mahayana Buddhists accept the Pali Canon as sacred scripture, but also many other writings or sutras, which were written later. While Theravada emphasizes individual enlightenment, Mahayana emphasizes the enlightenment of all beings. While the Theravada ideal is to become an arhat, the Mahayana ideal is to become a bodhisattva who strives to liberate all beings from the cycle of birth and death. Bodhisattvas enable all beings to be enlightened together, not only out of a sense of compassion, but because we cannot separate ourselves from each other. Mahayana Buddhists also teach that enlightenment can be attained in a single lifetime, and this can be accomplished even by a layperson.

- Adapted from the website (http://buddhism.about.com)

Fill in the Blanks

Mahayana Buddhism _____ in the first century CE. (부상하다)

Mahayana is a path available to people from all _____ of life. (모든 계층)

Mahayana Buddhism is predominant in the _____ _____. (극동)

Mahayana Buddhists also accept many other works or the _____, which were written later. (경전들)

Mahayana emphasizes the enlightenment of _____ _____.

(모든 존재)

The Mahayana ideal is to become a _____. (보살)

Bodhisattvas strive to _____ all beings. (해탈시키다)

Mahayana Buddhists teach that enlightenment can be attained in a

_____ _____. (한 생에)

Questions

1. When did Mahayana Buddhism emerge?

2. Does Mahayana have a more liberal interpretation of Buddhism?

3. Where can you find Mahayana Buddhism?

4. Is Mahayana also called "Northern Buddhism"?

5. Is Korea a Mahayana country?

6. What is the Mahayana ideal for human beings?

7. Do Mahayana Buddhists believe that enlightenment can be attained in a single lifetime?

Part 3

The History
and Culture of
Korean Buddhism
한국불교의 역사와 문화

1 대한불교조계종

조계종은 한국불교의 1700여 년 역사와 전통을 대표하는 종단이다.

조계종은 부처님의 가르침을 근본으로 직지인심(直指人心), 견성성불(見性成佛), 전법도생(傳法度生)을 종지로 하고 있다. 소의경전은 《금강경》《전등법어》이며, 참선수행을 근본으로 하면서도 간경과 염불, 주력 수행을 포용하여 통불교의 전통을 형성하고 있다. 특히, 조계종의 대표적인 '간화선 수행'은 세계인들이 주목하는 독특한 수행법이다. 25개의 불교종단 가운데 최대종단인 조계종은 전체 승려 수가 1만 2천여 명이고, 그중 약 1/5에 해당하는 2,200명의 스님들이 전통방식에 따라 90여 개의 선원에서 3개월 안거수행을 연중 두 차례 한다. 조계종의 종지종풍을 구현하는 사찰로는 5대 총림이 있다. 부처님의 경전을 배우는 승가대학은 19개로 1,700여 명의 출가자들이 공부하고 있다.

Unit 1 The Jogye Order of Korean Buddhism

The Jogye Order is the representative order of the Korean Buddhist tradition which has a history of more than 1700 years.

Its three foundation principles include: attaining awakening by the direct pointing to mind; attaining buddhahood by seeing the nature of mind; and saving sentient beings through dissemination of the Dharma. The order relies on the *Diamond Sutra* and the *Teachings of the Patriarchs* as its main scriptures. With Seon meditation as its pillar, the order embraces sutra study, chanting, and mantra recitation, to produce a syncretic Buddhism. In particular, Ganhwa Seon, the pre-eminent practice of the Jogye Order, has recently attracted world attention.

As the largest of more than 25 Buddhist orders in Korea, the Jogye Order has 12,000 monks and nuns. About one fifth of them (approx. 2,200) participate twice a year in the traditional, three-month meditation retreats called "angeo" which are held in 90 Seon halls nationwide.

There are five comprehensive training monasteries called "chongnim" which embody the monastic principles and traditions of the Jogye Order. There are 19 monastic academies in which 1,700 monastics study Buddhist scriptures.

The Jogye Order is the _____ order of the Korean Buddhist tradition.

(대표적인)

The Jogye Order's three _____ _____ include. (종지)

Attaining awakening by the _____ _____ to mind. (직지인심)

Attaining buddhahood by seeing the _____ of mind. (견성성불)

Saving sentient beings through _____ of the Dharma. (전법도생)

The Jogye Order relies on the *Diamond Sutra* and the *Teachings of the Patriarchs* as its _____ _____ . (소의경전)

With Seon meditation as its pillar, the order embraces sutra study, chanting, and mantra recitation, to produce a _____ _____ . (통불교)

In particular, _____ _____ , the pre-eminent practice of the Jogye Order, has recently attracted world attention. (간화선)

About _____ _____ of them (approx. 2,200) participate twice a year in the traditional, three-month meditation retreats called "angeo." (1/5)

1. Does the Korean Buddhist tradition have a history exceeding 1000 years?

2. What are the three foundation principles of the Jogye Order?

3. What are the two main scriptures of the Jogye Order?

4. Does the Jogye Order have Seon meditation as its core practice?

5. Does the Jogye Order only practice Seon meditation?

6. How many monks and nuns are there in the Jogye Order?

7. Does the majority of the Jogye Order participate in "angeo" every year?

8. How many comprehensive training monasteries does the Jogye Order have?

9. How many monastic academies are there in Korea?

❷ 불교의 전래

불교가 중국의 전진에서 도입된 것은 372년 또는 석가모니불이 입멸하신 지 800여 년 되던 해로, 이때 한국의 토속신앙은 샤머니즘이었다. 불교가 자연숭배 의식과 갈등관계가 없었기 때문에 샤머니즘과 조화를 이루며 한국에 정착하였다.

한국에서 불교를 최초로 받아들인 나라는 고구려로 소수림왕 2년에 중국 전진 왕 부견이 보낸 사문 순도가 불상과 경전을 가지고 왔다. 백제는 침류왕 원년(384)에 인도승 마라난타가 중국 동진에서 건너오면서 불교를 받아들였다. 왕이 교외에까지 나아가 그를 맞아들여 궁중에 머물게 하고 공경히 받들어 공양하며 그의 가르침을 받았다. 신라 불교 전래에는 여러 기록들이 혼재한다. 고구려에서 신라에 불교를 전한 인물로 승려 아도와 사문 묵호자 두 사람이 나타난다. 도입연도는 다양하게 나타나는데, 다음과 같다. 미추왕 2년(263), 눌지왕(417~458), 비처왕(479~499), 그리고 법흥왕 14년(527)이다. 하지만 공식적인 불교의 수용은 법흥왕(572년) 때 이차돈의 순교 사건을 계기로 이루어졌다.

💡 Unit 2 The Introduction of Buddhism into Korea

When Buddhism was originally introduced to Korea from China's Former Qin Dynasty in 372, about 800 years after the death of the historical Buddha, shamanism was Korea's indigenous faith. As Buddhism was not seen to conflict with the rites of nature worship, it was allowed to blend in with shamanism.

Korea's Goguryeo Kingdom first embraced Buddhism in the 2nd year of the reign of King Sosurim by welcoming Bhikkhu Shundao (Sundo), an envoy sent by King Fujian (Bugyeon) of the Former Qin (Jeonjin) Dynasty, who brought Buddha statues and sutras with him.

The Baekje Kingdom embraced Buddhism in 384, in the 1st year of the reign of King Chimnyu, by welcoming the Indian monk Marananta who had come from China's Eastern Jin Dynasty. King Chimnyu personally went to the outskirts of the capital to meet with Marananta, had him stay in the royal palace, and requested his teachings while providing for his needs.

The Silla Kingdom has contradictory records regarding the inception of Buddhism. Two different names appear as the Goguryeo envoy who introduced Buddhism, one being Bhikkhu Ado, and the other Sramana Mukhoja. The year of Buddhism's arrival in the Silla Kingdom also varies in historic records, some being: in 263 in the 2nd year of the reign of King Michu; during the reign of King Nulji (417~458); during the reign of King Bicheo (479~499); and in 527 in the 14th year of the reign of King Beopheung. However, official recognition of Buddhism was realized when the Silla monk, Lee Cha-don, was killed for his Buddhist beliefs during the reign of King Beopheung.

Fill in the Blanks

When Buddhism was originally _____ _____ Korea from China's Former Qin Dynasty in 372. (도입되다)

Shamanism was Korea's _____ _____. (토속신앙)

Korea's Goguryeo Kingdom first _____ Buddhism in the 2nd year of the reign of King Sosurim. (수용하다)

Bhikkhu Shundao (Sundo), an envoy sent by King Fujian (Bugyeon) of the Former Qin (Jeonjin) Dynasty, brought Buddha statues and _____ with him. (경전)

The Baekje Kingdom embraced Buddhism in 384, in the 1st year of the _____ of King Chimnyu. (재위)

The Baekje Kingdom welcomed the _____ _____ Marananta. (인도 스님)

King Chimnyu personally went to the outskirts of the _____ to meet with Marananta. (도성)

Two different names appear as the Goguryeo _____ who introduced Buddhism. (사절)

One being Bhikkhu Ado, and the other _____ Mukhoja. (사문)

However, _____ _____ of Buddhism was realized when the Silla monk, Lee Cha-don, was killed for his Buddhist beliefs. (공식 인가)

1. When was Buddhism first introduced to Korea?
2. What was Korea's indigenous faith around the time of Buddhism's introduction?
3. Who was the Goguryeo king who first embraced Buddhism?
4. Who brought Buddha statues and sutras to Goguryeo from the Former Qin Dynasty?
5. Was Marananta a Chinese monk?
6. When did Baekje embrace Buddhism?
7. When did Silla officially recognize Buddhism?

❸ 삼국 불교

삼국에서 불교를 받아들이는 데 앞장선 것은 모두 왕실이었다. 삼국이 강력한 왕권을 갖춘 국가로 성장하기 위해서는 그것을 뒷받침할 수 있는 새로운 이념과 정신적 지주가 필요했다. 그리하여 지배 체제의 유지에 불교를 이용하게 된다.

따라서 삼국시대의 불교는 호국적인 성격을 강하게 풍기게 되었다. 개인적인 치병이나 구복도 포함되지만 국가의 발전을 비는 호국신앙이 강렬하였다. 《인왕경》을 설하는 백좌강회(百座講會) 의식이 주기적으로 열려 국태민안의 기도를 하였다.

신라불교는 많은 고승대덕들을 배출하며 7~8세기에 황금기를 맞이하였다. 원광 법사는 삼국통일의 원동력이 된 화랑들에게 세속오계를 지키게 함으로써 정신적인 방향을 제시하였다. 특히 원효와 의상 스님이 이루어낸 눈부신 교학 연구는 중국불교에도 큰 영향을 주었고, 한국불교 발전의 주춧돌을 놓았다.

그러나 삼국시대 말기에는 이 같은 호국 신앙으로서의 불교도 변모하였다. 점차 내세를 기리는 신앙으로 바뀌어 간 것이다. 그리하여 미륵정토에 다시 나기를 기원하는 미륵 신앙이 널리 유행하였다.

🔔 Unit 3 Buddhism in Korea's Three Kingdoms

The royal courts took the initiative in embracing Buddhism in each of Korea's three kingdoms. In order for the kingdoms to develop as powerful states supported by strong royal power, they needed a new state ideology and a spiritual pillar, so they took advantage of Buddhism to maintain their system of rule.

Therefore, Buddhism during Korea's three kingdoms era was strongly characterized by the principle of state protection. Naturally there were also desires for the curing of disease and the receipt of personal blessings, but faith in state protection was upmost. Hundred-seat Dharma gatherings were regularly held to teach the *Sutra for Humane Kings* and to pray for national prosperity and the welfare of the people.

The Buddhism of Silla produced many eminent monks and ushered in a golden era which lasted from the 7th to 8th centuries. Ven. Wongwang provided spiritual direction by giving the Five Precepts for Laymen to a group of elite young men known as "Hwarang." In particular, the excellent doctrinal studies achieved by Ven. Wonhyo and Ven. Uisang had a great impact on Chinese Buddhism and laid the foundation for the development of Korean Buddhism.

However, at the end of the Korean three kingdoms era, the principle of state protection diminished in Korean Buddhism, and gradually Buddhism became a faith which believes in an afterlife. Thus, faith in Maitreya spread far and wide and people began to pray for rebirth into the Pure Land of Maitreya.

Fill in the Blanks

The royal courts _____ the _____ in embracing Buddhism in each of Korea's three kingdoms. (앞장서다)

They needed a new state ideology and a _____ _____.

(정신적 지주)

They took _____ of Buddhism to maintain their system of rule. (이용하다)

Therefore, Buddhism during Korea's three kingdoms era was strongly characterized by the principle of _____ _____. (호국)

Naturally there were also desires for the _____ of _____ and the receipt of personal blessings. (치병)

_____ Dharma gatherings were regularly held to teach the *Sutra for Humane Kings*. (백좌강회)

The Buddhism of Silla produced many _____ _____. (고승)

The Buddhism of Silla ushered in a _____ _____ which lasted from the 7th to 8th centuries. (황금기)

Ven. Wongwang provided spiritual direction by giving the Five Precepts for _____ to a group of elite young men. (세속오계)

In particular, the excellent _____ _____ achieved by Ven. Wonhyo and Ven. Uisang had a great impact on Chinese Buddhism. (교학)

However, at the end of the Korean three kingdoms era, Buddhism became a faith which believes in an _____ . (내세)

Thus, _____ in _____ spread far and wide and people began to pray for rebirth into the Pure Land of Maitreya. (미륵신앙)

Questions

1. Who took the initiative in embracing Buddhism in the three kingdoms of Korea?
2. How did Buddhism help in maintaining the ruling systems of the three kingdoms?
3. What did Buddhists pray for at the Hundred-seat Dharma gatherings?
4. When was Silla Buddhism's golden era?
5. What did Ven. Wongwang provide to guide young men?
6. Did Ven. Wonhyo have a great impact on Chinese Buddhism?
7. At the end of the Korean three kingdoms period, what did most people pray for?

4 이부승가 (비구, 비구니)

승가는 부처님을 따르던 불제자들이 2600년 전에 이룬 세계에서 가장 오래된 대중살이 사회라 할 수 있다. 한국에는 이미 1700년 전에 비구, 비구니 승가가 있었다는 기록이 존재한다. 한국은 여성 스님의 법맥을 인정하는 몇 안 되는 나라에 속한다. 불전에 의하면 비구니 종단은 최초의 수계 비구니가 된 부처님의 양어머니 마하파자파티 고타미의 특별한 요청에 의하여 설립되었다고 한다. 비록 현대에는 비구와 비구니가 비교적 동등한 대우를 받고 있지만 약간의 차이는 있다. 일상생활에서 비구니는 348계를 지켜야 하지만 비구는 250계를 지킨다. 2011년 10월 현재 조계종 전체 승려는 1만 2천여 명으로, 이 중 비구는 6천400여 명, 비구니는 5천600여 명이다.

Unit 4 The Dual Sangha of Bhikkhus and Bhikkhunis

The monastic sangha can be said to be the world's oldest communal society, dating back some 2600 years to the original followers of Sakyamuni Buddha. In Korea, there are records of ordained communities of monks and nuns dating back as far as 1700 years ago.

Korea is one of the few nations that recognize and continue female monastic lineages. According to Buddhist scriptures, the order of bhikkhunis was first created by the Buddha at the specific request of his foster-mother, Mahapajapati Gotami, who became the first ordained bhikkhuni. Though modern trends dictate that Buddhist nuns be treated relatively equally to monks, there are some differences between them. In daily life, bhikkhunis abide by nearly 348 precepts, while bhikkhus follow around 250.

As of October 2011, the Jogye Order has 12,000 monastics of which bhikkhus number 6,400 and bhikkhunis 5,600.

Fill in the Blanks

The monastic sangha can be said to be the world's oldest _____ _____ . (대중살이 사회)

Dating back some 2600 years to the original followers of _____ Buddha. (석가모니)

In Korea, there are _____ of ordained communities of monks and nuns dating back as far as 1700 years ago. (기록)

Korea is one of the few nations that recognize and continue _____ monastic lineages. (여성)

According to _____ _____ , the order of bhikkhunis was first created by the Buddha at the specific request of his foster-mother. (불전)

Mahapajapati Gotami became the first _____ bhikkhuni. (수계받은)

Modern trends dictate that Buddhist nuns be treated relatively _____ to monks. (동등하게)

In daily life, bhikkhunis _____ _____ nearly 348 precepts, while bhikkhus follow around 250. (준수하다)

As of October 2011, the Jogye Order has 12,000 monastics of which bhikkhus number 6,400 and _____ 5,600. (비구니)

Questions

1. Did the Sakyamuni Buddha have a monastic Sangha?
2. When was the first monastic Sangha established in Korea?
3. Are there many nations in the world which recognize bhikkhuni monastic lineages?
4. Who was the first bhikkhuni?
5. How many precepts do bhikkhus receive and observe?
6. How many precepts do bhikkhunis receive and observe?
7. How many bhikkhus and bhikkhunis does the Jogye Order have as of October 2011?

조계종 전통에서는 스님이 되고자 하는 사람은 구족계를 받기까지 3단계를 거친다. 계를 받기 전에 6~12개월의 수습기간을 거쳐야 하는데, 이를 행자라고 한다. 행자는 계행을 배우고 불교의식과 사찰 예절을 익힌다. 행자는 또한 절에서 대중생활에 필요한 많은 운력(일: 육체적 노동)을 한다. 이런 수련은 사찰의 생활풍습을 익힘과 아울러 세속에서의 인연을 잊고 스님으로서 새로 태어나기 위한 과정이다.

소정의 행자생활을 마치면 사미계나 사미니계를 받게 되는데, 요즘은 종단에서 마련한 단일계단인 수계산림에서 소정의 교육을 받고 엄격한 심사를 거쳐야 한다. 사미·사미니는 승가대학이나 선원 등에서 보다 전문적인 교육을 받으며, 이러한 과정을 거쳐 승납 4년 이상 연령 20세 이상이 되어야 비구계나 비구니계를 받을 자격이 된다.

Unit 5 **How to Become a Buddhist Monk or Nun**

In the tradition of the Jogye Order, an aspirant goes through three steps to become a fully ordained monk or nun. One needs to spend 6~12 months in a probationary period as a postulant (haengja) before taking the novice precepts. Postulants learn moral discipline, as well as basic Buddhist cermonies and temple manners. They also spend most of their time doing physical work in the service of the temple. This training is required to acquaint them with the monastic lifestyle, and to be reborn as a monastic Buddhist by severing their connections to the secular life.

Upon successful completion of postulant training, a postulant takes the novice precepts to become a novice monk (Skt. śrāmaṇera; Pali sāmaṇera) or novice nun (Skt. śrāmaṇerikā; Pali sāmaṇeri). Currently, the Jogye Order establishes a single ordination platform at a designated temple. Candidates receive a prescribed education in this temple and are ordained as novices after strict evaluation.

Novices receive more specialized education in one of the monastic academies or Seon halls. After finishing this training course, a novice who is older than 20 and has spent more than four years as an ordained monastic is eligible to take the full precepts to become a fully ordained monk (Skt. bhikṣu; Pali bhikkhu) or nun (Skt. bhikṣuṇī; Pali bhikkhunī).

In the tradition of the Jogye Order, an aspirant goes through _____ _____ to become a fully ordained monk or nun. (삼단계)

One needs to spend 6~12 months in a _____ _____ as a postulant (haengja) before taking the novice precepts. (수습기간)

Postulants learn moral discipline, as well as basic _____ _____ and temple manners. (불교의식)

They also spend most of their time doing _____ _____ in the service of the temple. (육체적 노동)

This training is required to acquaint them with the _____ _____ .
(사찰 생활풍습)

This training is required to be _____ as a monastic Buddhist. (거듭나다)

By _____ their connections to the secular life. (끊다)

Upon successful completion of postulant training, a postulant takes the _____ _____ to become a novice monk or nun. (사미계 · 사미니계)

Currently, the Jogye Order establishes a single _____ _____ at a designated temple. (계단)

Candidates receive a _____ education in this temple. (소정의)

Candidates are ordained as novices after _____ _____ .
(엄격한 심사)

Novices receive more _____ education in one of the monastic academies or Seon halls. (전문적인)

He is _____ to take the precepts. (자격이 있는)

He took the _____ _____ to become a fully ordained monk. (구족계)

Questions

1. How many steps does an aspirant go through in order to become a fully ordained monastic in the Jogye Order?
2. How long is the trial period for postulants (haengja)?
3. Do postulants learn basic Buddhist ceremonies?
4. Does the Jogye Order operate a single ordination platform?
5. Do the ordination candidates receive a prescribed education before taking the novice and full precepts?
6. Can a novice practice in a Seon hall as part of the qualification for taking the full precepts?
7. Can a 19-year-old novice take the full precepts?

6 안거

한국불교에는 간화선이라는 수행법 전통이 있다. 간화선은 다른 불교 전통에서는 별로 찾아볼 수 없는 독특한 참선법이다. 매년 조계종에는 2000여 명의 선승들이 여름과 겨울 각 3개월씩 안거에 들어간다. '편안히 머문다'는 뜻의 안거는 대중들이 '규칙을 준수한다'는 의미의 결제로 시작되며, 안거 중에 수행자들은 산문을 나가지 않고 참선과 기타 수행에 전념한다. 이들의 일과는 새벽 3시에 시작되고 어떤 경우는 2시에도 시작된다. 안거가 끝나면 참선 수행자들은 '만행'이라 불리는 행각을 떠난다. 만행의 목적은 이들이 안거 중 배운 것을 실생활에서 구현하는 데 있다.

Unit 6 Summer and Winter Retreats

In Korean Buddhism, one finds a legacy of Ganhwa Seon practice, a unique method of Seon meditation rarely found in other Buddhist traditions.

In the Jogye Order, over 2,000 monks and nuns attend three-month-long summer and winter retreats every year in Seon monasteries and nunneries. During a retreat, called "angeo" (lit. to reside in peace) that starts with "gyeolje" (lit. binding rule), practitioners devote themselves to Seon meditation and other practices without leaving the temple. Their daily routine starts at 3 a.m. and in some cases at 2 a.m.

When the retreat ends, Seon practitioners leave to carry out a "traveling practice" called "manhaeng" (lit. ten thousand actions). The purpose of manhaeng is to apply in real life situations what they have learned while meditating during the retreat.

Fill in the Blanks

In Korean Buddhism, one finds a _____ of Ganhwa Seon practice. (전통)

Ganhwa Seon is a unique method of Seon meditation _____ found in other Buddhist traditions. (드물게)

Over 2,000 monks and nuns _____ three-month-long summer and winter retreats every year in Seon monasteries and nunneries. (참가하다)

"Angeo" literally means to reside _____ _____ . (편안히)

"Gyeolje" literally means _____ _____ . (규칙을 준수하다)

During a retreat, _____ devote themselves to Seon meditation and other practices without leaving the temple. (수행자들)

Their _____ _____ starts at 3 a.m. and in some cases at 2 a.m.

(일과)

When the retreat _____ , Seon practitioners leave to carry out a "traveling practice." (끝나다)

"Manhaeng" literally means ten thousand _____ . (행)

The _____ of manhaeng is to apply in _____ _____ situations what they have learned while meditating during the retreat.

(목적) (실생활)

Questions

1. What is the legacy of Seon meditation found in Korea?
2. How long is the summer retreat called "ha-angeo"?
3. How many monastics participate in the summer and winter retreats?
4. Should monastics remain within the temple compound during retreats?
5. What time does the daily schedule begin during the retreat?
6. What is the "traveling practice" called in Korean?
7. What is the purpose of the traveling practice?

7 부처님오신날

부처님오신날은 지역에 따라 약간의 차이가 있다. 아시아 대부분 지역에서는 음력 4월 첫째 보름날에 축하하지만, 한국에서의 부처님오신날은 언제나 음력 4월 초파일(4월 8일)이다.

상좌부불교에서는 부처님의 탄신일, 성도일, 열반일을 하나로 합쳐 '웨삭'에 지내는 반면 대승불교에서는 대체로 이 세 날을 따로 기념한다.

부처님오신날은 연등을 걸고 함께 대중 공양을 하며, 악사, 무용가, 장식차 등의 행렬은 아시아 전역에서 보이는 일반적인 모습이다. 아시아 불교국가의 공통적인 의례는 아기부처님의 관욕이다. 사람들은 경건하게 불단에 다가가 작은 바가지에 물이나 차를 채워서 아기부처님 머리 위에 부어 관욕을 시킨다.

부처님오신날은 한국불교에서 가장 큰 명절이다. 이 날을 한국어로 '부처님오신날'이라 부른다. 이때쯤 절과 거리는 연등으로 가득 차게 된다.

Unit 7 Buddha's Birthday

Buddha's Birthday is celebrated on different dates in different regions. In most of Asia, it is observed on the full moon of the fourth month of the lunar calendar. In Korea, Buddha's Birthday always falls on April 8 by the lunar calendar.

Theravada Buddhists combine the observance of Buddha's birth, his enlightenment and his passing-away into one holiday called Vesak, while most Mahayana Buddhists observe these as three separate holidays held at different times of the year.

Buddha's Birthday is a time for hanging lanterns and enjoying communal meals. Joyous parades of musicians, dancers and floats are common throughout Asia. One ritual found throughout Buddhist countries in Asia is that of washing the baby Buddha. People approach the altar reverently, fill a ladle with water or tea, and pour it over a statue of the baby Buddha.

Buddha's Birthday is the biggest Buddhist holiday in Korea. In Korea this day is called "Bucheonim osin nal" meaning "the day when the Buddha came." Lotus lanterns cover entire temples and nearby streets throughout the month.

Buddha's Birthday is celebrated on _____ _____ in different regions. (다른 날)

In most of Asia, it is observed on the _____ _____ of the fourth month of the lunar calendar. (보름)

In Korea, Buddha's Birthday always falls on April 8 by the _____ _____ . (음력)

Theravada Buddhists combine the observance of Buddha's birth, his enlightenment and his passing-away into one holiday called _____ . (웨삭)

Most _____ Buddhists observe these as three separate holidays held at different times of the year. (대승)

Buddha's Birthday is a time for _____ _____ . (등을 걸다)

Buddha's Birthday is also a time for enjoying _____ _____ .

(대중 공양)

Joyous parades of musicians, dancers and _____ are common throughout Asia. (장식차)

One ritual found throughout Asia is that of _____ the baby Buddha.

(목욕시키다)

People approach the _____ reverently. (불단)

People _____ water or tea over a statue of the baby Buddha. (붓는다)

Buddha's Birthday is the _____ Buddhist holiday in Korea. (최대의)

"Bucheonim osin nal" means "the day when the Buddha _____." (오신)

Lotus lanterns cover entire temples and _____ _____ throughout the month. (인근 거리)

Questions
1. Is Buddha's Birthday celebrated on the same day throughout the world?
2. Are Buddha's Birthday and Bodhi Day celebrated together in Korea?
3. Did you hang lanterns on this past Buddha's Birthday?
4. Did you go see the lantern parade on this past Buddha's Birthday?
5. Do Buddhist devotees wash the baby Buddha on Buddha's Birthday?
6. Is Buddha's Birthday the second biggest Buddhist holiday in Korea?
7. What does "Bucheonim osin nal" mean?

8 스님의 하루일과 1

3시 기상

산사의 하루는 다른 곳보다 일찍 시작된다. 불자들은 산사에서 새벽 3시에 목탁 소리에 맞추어 기상을 한다. 목탁 소리는 모든 중생을 잠에서 깨운다는 의미를 가지고 있다.

새벽 예불

새벽 예불은 불보살님께 예경을 올리는 의식이다. 예불 시 스님들은 가사를 갖추어 입는다. 일반적으로 절에서 거주하는 모든 사람들은 새벽 예불에 참가해야 한다.

발우공양

절에서의 식사를 '공양'이라고 한다. 아침 식사는 대체로 6시에 먹는다. 한국의 스님들은 대체로 식사를 발우공양으로 한다. 각 수행자는 '발우'라 불리는 네 개의 목발우 그릇을 사용한다. 각자 먹을 만큼만 그릇에 담는다. 전통 사찰 식사법인 발우공양은 생명을 소중히 여기고 환경을 보존하는 의미를 담고 있다.

Unit 8 A Day in a Mountain Temple I

Wake up at 3 AM

The day begins earlier in mountain temples than in the rest of the world. Buddhists wake up at 3 a.m. in mountain temples at the sound of the moktak (wooden handbell), which is meant to awaken all beings from the sleep of ignorance.

Early Morning Buddhist Ceremony (Yebul)

The early morning ceremony is held to pay homage to buddhas and bodhisattvas. Buddhist monks and nuns are fully dressed in monastic garb, including ceremonial robes called "kasaya," for this ceremony. Generally, all temple residents are required to attend the morning ceremony.

Formal Monastic Meal (Baru Gongyang)

Temple meals are called "gongyang" in Korean, meaning "offering." Breakfast is usually eaten around 6 a.m. Korean Buddhist monks and nuns usually have their meals in the style of "baru gongyang." Each monastic uses a set of four wooden bowls called baru. They serve themselves only as much as they can eat. The traditional monastic meal, baru gongyang, embodies the spirit of cherishing life and of preserving the environment.

Fill in the Blanks

The day begins _____ in mountain temples than in the rest of the world.

(더 일찍)

Buddhists wake up at 3 a.m. in _____ _____ at the sound of the moktak. (산사)

The sound of the moktak is meant to _____ all beings from the sleep of ignorance. (깨우다)

The early morning ceremony is held to pay _____ to buddhas and bodhisattvas. (예경)

Buddhist monks and nuns are _____ _____ in monastic garb, including ceremonial robes called "kasaya," for this ceremony. (옷을 갖추어 입다)

Generally, all temple _____ are required to attend the morning ceremony.

(거주자)

"Gongyang" means "_____." (공양)

Breakfast is usually eaten _____ 6 a.m. (경에)

Korean Buddhist monks and nuns usually have their _____ in the style of "baru gongyang." (식사, 공양)

Each monastic uses a set of four _____ _____ called baru. (목발우)

They serve themselves only as _____ _____ they can eat. (~만큼)

The traditional monastic meal, baru gongyang, embodies the _____ of cherishing life and of preserving the environment. (정신)

Questions

1. What time do monastics wake up in mountain temples?
2. What is the sound of the wooden handbell meant for?
3. What is the early morning ceremony offered for?
4. Do Buddhist monastics wear kasaya for early morning ceremonies?
5. What does "gongyang" mean?
6. How many wooden bowls are there in a baru set?
7. In what spirit do monastics have baru gongyang?

175

9 스님의 하루일과 2

운력

절에서는 대중들이 함께 모여 하는 육체적 노동인 운력(運力)이 있다. 운력은 선불교도에게 는 중요한 수행 방법이며, 모든 사람이 참석한다. "하루 일하지 않으면 하루 먹지 않겠다." 는 백장 선사의 가르침은 수행과 노동이 둘이 아니라는 사실을 말해준다. 절을 청소하는 것 은 마음을 깨끗이 하는 것과 같다. 운력을 통해 스님들은 절을 청소하고, 이불과 방석을 빨 고, 채마밭을 가꾼다.

공부와 수행

스님들은 오전, 오후, 저녁 시간에 공부와 수행을 한다. 승가대학에 재학 중인 스님들은 부 처님의 가르침을 공부하고, 선원에서 수학하는 스님들은 참선 수행을 한다.

취침

대중살이를 하는 스님들은 주로 저녁 9시에 소등을 한 후 잠자리에 든다. 잠들기 전에 그들 은 하루를 되돌아본다. 하루를 잘 보냈다면 쌓은 공덕을 모든 중생의 깨달음을 위해 회향한 다. 만약 성실하게 보내지 못했다면 반성을 하고 다시는 그런 행동을 하지 않겠다고 다짐한 다. 하지만 모든 스님들이 다 9시에 잠자리에 드는 것은 아니다. 밤새워 수행정진하는 스님 들도 있다.

Unit 9 A Day in a Mountain Temple II

Communal Work (Ullyeok)

In the temple, after breakfast, there is communal work called "ullyeok." Communal work is an important practice for Seon Buddhists and is done by everyone. "No work, no food," the words of Chinese Seon Master Baizhang, confirms that Buddhist practice and physical work are not separate.

Cleaning the temple is like cleaning the mind. During communal work, monastics clean the temple, wash blankets and cushions, and cultivate vegetable gardens.

Study and Practice

Buddhist monks and nuns study and practice in the mornings, afternoons and evenings. In the monastic academy, monastics study the teachings of the

Buddha. In the Seon halls, monastics practice Seon meditation.

Going to Bed

Most monastics in a communal living environment turn off the lights at 9 p.m. and go to bed. Before retiring for the night, monastics examine their day's behavior. If they acted well, they dedicate the merit thus gained to the enlightenment of all beings. If they acted improperly, they repent and vow to never again engage in such negative actions. However, not all monastics go to bed at 9 p.m. Some monks and nuns practice all night.

Fill in the Blanks

In the temple there is _____ _____ called "ullyeok." (대중 노동)

Communal work is an important _____ for Seon Buddhists. (수행)

"No work, no food" is the _____ of Chinese Seon Master Baizhang. (말씀)

It confirms that Buddhist practice and physical work are not _____.

(분리된, 별개의)

Cleaning the temple is like cleaning the _____. (마음)

During communal work, monastics _____ blankets. (세탁하다)

They wash _____. (좌복)

They _____ vegetable gardens. (가꾸다)

Buddhist monks and nuns _____ and practice in the mornings, afternoons and evenings. (공부하다)

In the monastic academy, monastics study the _____ of the Buddha.

(가르침)

In the Seon halls, monastics practice _____ _____. (참선)

Most monastics in a communal living environment _____ _____ the lights at 9 p.m. (끄다)

Before retiring for the night, monastics _____ their day's behavior.

(점검하다)

If they acted well, they dedicate the _____ thus gained to the enlightenment of all beings. (공덕)

If they acted improperly, they _____. (참회하다)

They vow to never again engage in such _____ actions. (부정적인)

Some monks and nuns practice _____ _____. (밤새도록)

Questions

1. Is communal work part of Buddhist practice in Seon temples?
2. What are the famous Seon words offered by the Chinese Seon Master Baizhang?
3. Are Buddhist practice and physical work different for Seon monks and nuns?
4. Do monastics study the teachings of the Buddha in a monastic academy?
5. Do Buddhist monks and nuns perform prostration practice?
6. What time do monastics go to bed?
7. Do all monastics go to bed at a set bedtime?

10 스님들의 활동 1

참선

내 한 생각의 일어나고 사라짐이 곧 우주의 건립과 파괴요, 인생의 생사니라.   – 만공 스님

참선(參禪)은 화두를 일념으로 참구하는 것으로 불교의 대표적인 수행법이다. 참선은 지혜와 깨달음의 체득을 그 목표로 한다. 선은 중국에 최초로 참선법을 전한 달마 조사에서 유래한다고 알려져 있다. 한국에서는 많은 사찰들이 참선 수행을 위한 선원(禪院)을 운영하고 있으며, 여름과 겨울에는 석 달씩 결제 정진하기도 한다.

참선 수행자의 수행 정도를 가늠하고 지도하기 위해 스승과의 면담이 있다. 이를 선문답이라 한다. 전해지는 조사 어록으로 《임제록》, 《벽암록》, 《조주록》 등이 유명하다.

간경

간경은 경전을 통해 불법을 공부하는 방법 중 하나이다. 간경은 소리를 내어 반복해서 읽거나 묵묵히 경의 내용을 음미하고 분석하는 것이다. 참선 수행자가 온 신경을 화두에 쏟듯이 경의 구절을 세심하게 정독(精讀)하는 것이다.

《선가귀감》에서 서산 대사는 "경을 보면서 마음속을 향해 공부하지 않는다면, 만 권의 글을 모두 보아도 아무런 이익이 없다."고 하였다. 육조 혜능 역시 《법화경》을 외우는 데 주력하던 제자 법달에게 경전의 속뜻을 깨달아야 한다고 충고하였다.

Unit 10 Activities of Monastics I

Seon meditation

With the arising and ceasing of a thought comes the establishment and destruction of the universe; or the birth and death of human life.

- Ven. Mangong

Seon meditation is an important method of Buddhist practice which single-mindedly investigates a "hwadu." Seon meditation aims for the attainment of wisdom and enlightenment. Seon is known to have originated with the Patriarch Bodhidharma who first introduced Seon meditation to China.

In Korea, many temples operate Seon halls for the practice of Seon meditation. They have three-month retreats in the summer and winter for intensive meditation practice.

In order to estimate the progress of Seon practitioners and give them proper guidance, teachers interview the practitioners. The content of this interview is called a Seon dialogue. There are writings containing the Seon dialogues of former Patriarchs, such as The *Record of Linji* (臨濟錄; *Linjilu*), *Blue Cliff Record* (碧巖錄; *Biyanlu*), and *The Record of Zhaozhou* (趙州錄; *Zhaozhoulu*).

Sutra Reading (Gangyeong)

"Sutra reading" or gangyeong is one method to study the Buddha-dharma. Gangyeong is to read a sutra repeatedly and aloud or to ponder, analyze and closely study the content of the sutras. Practitioners of gangyeong read each phrase of the sutra in silence with the greatest care, just as Seon practitioners focus their whole attention on their hwadu.

Master Seosan said, in the *Mirror for Seon Students* (禪家龜鑑; *Seonga Gwigam*), "If you don't cultivate your mind while reading sutras, even the reading of 10,000 sutras won't bring any benefit." The Sixth Patriarch Huineng advised his disciple Fada, who was dedicated to memorizing the *Lotus Sutra*, to realize the inner meaning of the sutra.

Fill in the Blanks

With the _____ and _____ of a thought comes the establishment and destruction of the universe. (일어나고 사라짐)

Seon meditation is an important _____ of Buddhist practice. (방법)

Seon meditation _____ investigates a "hwadu." (일심으로)

Seon meditation aims for the _____ of wisdom and enlightenment. (증득)

Seon is known to have _____ with the Patriarch Bodhidharma. (발원하다)

In Korea, many temples operate _____ _____ for the practice of Seon meditation. (선원)

They have three-month retreats in the summer and winter for _____ meditation practice. (집중적인)

In order to estimate the _____ of Seon practitioners and give them proper guidance, teachers _____ the practitioners. (발전, 면담하다)

The content of this interview is called a _____ _____ . (선문답)

"Sutra reading" is one method to study the _____ . (불법)

Gangyeong is to read a sutra repeatedly and _____ . (소리내어)

It is to ponder, _____ , and closely study the content of the sutras. (분석하다)

Practitioners of gangyeong read each phrase of the sutra _____ _____ with the greatest care. (조용히, 소리 없이)

Just as Seon practitioners focus their whole _____ on their hwadu. (주의)

Even the reading of 10,000 sutras won't bring any _____ . (득, 혜택)

The _____ _____ Huineng advised his disciple Fada. (육조)

Tang Dynasty monk Fada was dedicated to _____ the *Lotus Sutra*. (암기하다)

To realize the _____ _____ of the sutra. (속뜻)

Questions
1. What does Seon meditation investigate?
2. What does Seon meditation aim for?
3. Where did Seon meditation originate?
4. Why do teachers interview Seon practitioners?
5. Name one record of Seon dialogues.
6. Do Buddhist monks and nuns only read sutras to study the Buddha-dharma?
7. What was Master Seosan's admonition for those who read sutras?

181

11 스님들의 활동 2

포교

포교는 2600여 년 전 석가모니 부처님으로부터 시작되었다. 부처님은 수행자들에게 모든 중생을 행복하고 이롭게 하기 위해 마음을 닦으라고 하셨다.

법을 나누는 것은, 도심 사찰이나 산중사찰에서든, 스님들이 해야 할 책임 중 하나이다. 법을 가르치는 것은 보시의 실천이고 이는 모든 생명을 이롭게 하려는 자비로운 마음에서 비롯된다. 포교는 1962년 조계종이 공식출범할 때 설정한 3대 목표 중 하나이기도 하다.

포교의 노력 덕분에 불법은 한국에 1700여 년 동안 존재하였다. 법문과 법회는 포교의 수단이다. 재가자의 교육 역시 포교의 일환이다. 최근 한국에서는 재가자를 위한 '불교대학'이 활발히 운영되고 있다. 지난 몇십 년 동안 이 대학들은 수십만 명의 졸업생을 배출했다.

사회 복지

일부 스님들은 깨달음을 얻고 모든 중생을 고통에서 건지려는 수행의 일환으로 사회복지에 종사하기도 한다. 어떤 방법으로든 남을 돕는 것을 목적으로 하는 다양한 사업을 한국 스님들은 펼치고 있다. 불교계는 현재 550여 개의 복지시설을 운영하고 있고 이곳에 만여 명의 직원이 종사하고 있다. 복지시설에는 양로원, 지역센터, 탁아소 등이 있다.

불교계는 또한 인권, 통일, 생태, 여성의 권리, 노동자의 권리 등에 관련된 일을 하는 많은 사회사업기관과 NGO단체를 지원한다. 이런 단체로는 정토회, 지구촌공생회, 로터스 월드, 조계종사회복지재단 등이 있다.

Unit 11 Activities of Monastics II

Dharma Propagation

Dharma propagation began with Sakyamuni Buddha almost 2600 years ago. He encouraged practitioners to cultivate spiritual development for the benefit and happiness of all beings.

Sharing the Dharma, whether in city temples or mountain temples, is one responsibility of monastics. Teaching the Dharma is a practice of generosity which arises from a compassionate wish to benefit all living beings. Dharma propagation was also one of the three main goals of the Jogye Order of Korean Buddhism when it was officially established in 1962.

Thanks to the efforts of Dharma propagation, the Dharma has been in Korea for almost 1700 years. Dharma teachings and Dharma gatherings are a means of Dharma propagation. The education of lay people is another venue of Dharma propagation. Recently in Korea, the "Buddhist College" for the laity has been a big success. This very popular program has seen hundreds of thousands of graduates over the last few decades.

Social Work

Some monks and nuns engage in social work as part of their practice to gain enlightenment and save all beings from suffering. With a primary focus on helping others in whatever way possible, Korean monastics have set up a variety of programs. There are over 550 Buddhist social welfare facilities with over 10,000 workers, some of which are nursing homes, community centers, day care centers, etc.

The Buddhist community also supports many social organizations and NGOs involved in human rights, Korean unification, ecology, women's rights, and the rights of workers. These NGOs include the Jungto Society, Good Hands, Lotus World, and the Jogye Order Social Welfare Foundation.

Fill in the Blanks

_____ _____ began with Sakyamuni Buddha almost 2600 years ago. (포교)

He encouraged practitioners to cultivate spiritual development for the benefit and _____ of all beings. (행복)

Sharing the Dharma, whether in city temples or mountain temples, is one _____ of monastics. (책임)

Teaching the Dharma is a practice of _____ . (보시)

It arises from a _____ wish to benefit all living beings. (자비로운)

Dharma propagation was also one of the three main goals of the Jogye Order of Korean Buddhism when it _____ officially _____ in 1962. (창립되다, 출범하다)

_____ _____ the efforts of Dharma propagation, the Dharma has been in Korea for almost 1700 years. (덕분에)

Dharma teachings and Dharma gatherings are a _____ of Dharma propagation. (수단, 방법)

Recently in Korea, the "Buddhist College" for the _____ has been a big success. (재가자)

This very popular program has seen hundreds of thousands of _____ over the last few decades. (졸업생)

Some monks and nuns engage in _____ _____ as part of their practice. (복지 사업)

With a _____ _____ on helping others in whatever way possible, Korean monastics have set up a variety of programs. (주된 관심사)

There are over 550 Buddhist social welfare _____ with over 10,000 workers. (시설)

Some of which are nursing homes, _____ _____ centers, etc. (탁아소)

The Buddhist community also supports many social organizations and NGOs involved in _____ _____, Korean unification, ecology. (인권)

These NGOs include the Jungto Society, Good Hands, and the Jogye Order Social Welfare _____. (재단)

Questions
1. What did the Buddha encourage Buddhist practitioners to cultivate?
2. Is sharing the Dharma only a responsibility of monastics in city temples?
3. Is Dharma propagation one of the three main goals of the Jogye Order?
4. Are both Dharma teachings and social work a means of Dharma propagation?
5. How many Buddhist social welfare facilities are there in Korea?
6. Is protecting human rights a cause of Buddhist social work?
7. Does the Jogye Order Social Welfare Foundation conduct a broad scope of social work?

12 전각 1

대웅전

석가모니 부처님을 주불로 모신 법당이다. 절의 중심이 되는 전각으로 대부분의 주요 행사는 모두 대웅전에서 열린다. 대웅전은 '법력으로 세상을 밝히는 부처님(위대한 영웅)을 모신 전각'이라는 뜻이다.

대웅전에는 본존불인 석가모니불의 좌우에 협시하는 분으로 문수보살과 보현보살 또는 가섭존자와 아난존자를 모신다. 때로 삼세불이나 삼신불을 모시기도 한다. 삼세불은 현세의 석가모니불, 과거의 연등불인 제화갈라보살, 그리고 미래불인 미륵보살이다. 삼신불은 법신불, 보신불, 화신불이다.

대적광전

대적광전의 본존불인 비로자나불은 '편재하는 광명'을 나타낸다. 지혜가 어디든지 편재하는 비로자나불은 화엄종의 주된 상징이기도 하다. 비로자나불의 세계가 진리의 빛으로 가득하고 고요하다 하여 대적광전이라 부른다. 대적광전에는 비로자나불을 주불로 하고 아미타불, 석가모니불을 봉안하는 게 상례다.

Unit 12 Temple Shrines I

The Main Buddha Hall (Daeung-jeon)

The Main Buddha Hall enshrines Sakyamuni Buddha as the principal buddha. As the central building of the temple, most of the important Dharma gatherings take place in this hall. Its name "Daeung-jeon" means "the hall that enshrines the hero who illuminates the world with his spiritual power."

Inside the Buddha Hall, Sakyamuni Buddha is flanked by the Samantabhadra Bodhisattva (Bohyeon Bosal) and the Manjusri Bodhisattva (Munsu Bosal); or by Ven. Kasyapa and Ven. Ananda. Sometimes the "Buddhas of the three times" (past, present and future) or the "three bodies of the Buddha" are enshrined. The Buddhas of the three times are: Sakyamuni Buddha of the present, Dipankara Buddha of the past, and Maitreya Buddha of the future. The Buddhas of the three bodies are the Dharmakaya Buddha, Sambhogakaya Buddha, and Nirmanakaya Buddha.

The Vairocana Hall (Daejeok-gwangjeon or Biro-jeon)

As the principal buddha of the Vairocana Hall, Vairocana Buddha represents "universal illumination." This Buddha, whose wisdom penetrates everywhere, is a major symbol of the Hwaeom (Chi. Huayan) School. The hall is also called "Hall of Great Silence and Light" as the world of Vairocana is filled with the light of truth.

In the Vairocana Hall, it is common to enshrine the Vairocana Buddha as the principal buddha with Amitabha Buddha and Sakyamuni Buddha as attendants.

Fill in the Blanks

The Main Buddha Hall _____ Sakyamuni Buddha as the principal buddha.

(모시다)

As the central building of the temple, most of the important Dharma gatherings _____ _____ in this hall. (일어나다)

"Daeung-jeon" means "the hall that enshrines the _____ who illuminates the world with his spiritual power." (영웅)

Sakyamuni Buddha is _____ by the Samantabhadra Bodhisattva (Bohyeon Bosal) and the Manjusri Bodhisattva (Munsu Bosal). (옆에서 모시다, 호위하다)

Sometimes the "Buddhas of the _____ _____" (past, present and future) or the "_____ _____ of the Buddha" are enshrined. (삼세) (삼신)

The Buddhas of the three times are: Sakyamuni Buddha of the present, _____ Buddha of the past, and Maitreya Buddha of the future. (연등불, 제화갈라보살)

As the _____ _____ of the Vairocana Hall, (본존불)

Vairocana Buddha represents "_____ _____." (편재하는 광명)

Vairocana Buddha is a major _____ of the Hwaeom (Chi. Huayan) School. (상징)

The hall is also called "Hall of _____ _____ and Light" (대적)

In the Vairocana Hall, it is common to enshrine the Vairocana Buddha as the principal buddha with _____ _____ and Sakyamuni Buddha as attendants. (아미타불)

Questions

1. Who is usually enshrined in the Main Buddha Hall?
2. Where do most of the important Dharma gatherings take place in temples?
3. What does "Daeung-jeon" mean?
4. What is the Buddha triad that is most often found enshrined in the Main Buddha Hall?
5. What does Vairocana Buddha represent?
6. Which Buddhist school is Vairocana Buddha closely associated with?
7. In the Vairocana Hall, who are the attendant buddhas?

전각 2

관음전(원통전)

여기는 관세음보살을 모신 곳이다. 자비의 보살인 관
세음보살은 한국과 대승불교에서 가장 대중적인 보살
이다. 관음은 동아시아에서 대체로 여성으로 묘사되
며 한없는 자비심을 지닌 것으로 알려져 있다. '관세
음'이라는 말은 '세상의 소리를 관하는 자'를 의미한
다. 즉 도움이 필요한 사람들의 외침에 응해준다는 말
이다. 관세음은 때로 천 개의 눈과 천 개의 손을 가진
것으로 묘사되는데 이는 중생의 고통을 도우려는 커
다란 원력을 상징한다.

명부전(지장전)

명부전은 지장보살을 모신 곳이다. 지장보살은 대서
원의 보살, 지옥의 보살, 내세의 보살 등으로 불린다.
지장보살은 모든 중생이 지옥에서 벗어날 때까지 열
반에 들지 않겠다고 서원을 했다. 한국의 전통신앙에
의하면 사자(死者)는 시왕(十王) 앞에서 심판을 받는다.
지장보살은 이들 사자들을 구하고 중음상태에 있을
때, 그리고 지하세계에서 길을 잃었을 때 이들을 보호
한다.

Unit 13 Temple Shrines II

Avalokitesvara Hall (Gwaneum-jeon or Wontong-jeon)

This hall is dedicated to Avalokitesvara Bodhisattva. Avalokitesvara
(Gwanseeum Bosal), the Bodhisattva of compassion, is the most popular
figure in Korean and Mahayana Buddhism. Avalokitesvara is generally
depicted as female in East Asia and is known for her infinite compassion. Her
name translates as "one who observes/regards the sounds of the world." That
is, she responds to the cries of those in need of help. She is sometimes

depicted with a thousand hands and eyes which are symbolic of her great desire to help the suffering of sentient beings.

Judgment Hall (Myeongbu-jeon or Jijang-jeon)

This hall is dedicated to Ksitigarbha Bodhisattva (Jijang Bosal). In English he is variously called: the Earth-Storehouse Bodhisattva, the Bodhisattva of Great Vows, the Bodhisattva of Hell, or the Bodhisattva of the Afterlife. Ksitigarbha has sworn not to enter nirvana until every being is freed from hell. According to Korean folk beliefs, the deceased pass before ten kings to be judged. Ksitigarbha acts on their behalf to ensure salvation and protects them while they are in the intermediate state between death and rebirth, as well as those lost in the underworld.

Fill in the Blanks

Gwaneum-jeon is _____ to Avalokitesvara Bodhisattva. (헌정하다, 모시다)

Avalokitesvara (Gwanseeum Bosal) is the Bodhisattva of _____. (자비)

Avalokitesvara is generally depicted as _____ in East Asia. (여성)

Avalokitesvara is known for her _____ compassion. (무한한)

Her name translates as "one who _____ / _____ the sounds of the world." (관하다 / 주목하다)

She responds to the _____ of those in need of help. (외침)

She is sometimes depicted with a thousand _____ and _____.
(천수천안)

Ksitigarbha Bodhisattva is variously called: the Earth-Storehouse Bodhisattva, the Bodhisattva of _____ _____, the Bodhisattva of Hell, or the Bodhisattva of the _____. (대원) (내세)

Ksitigarbha has sworn not to _____ _____ until every being is freed from hell. (열반에 들다)

According to Korean folk beliefs, the _____ pass before _____ _____ to be judged. (사자) (시왕)

Ksitigarbha protects them while they are in the _____ _____ , as well as those lost in the _____ . (중음) (지하세계)

Questions

1. What is Avalokitesvara Bodhisattva known for?
2. Is Avalokitesvara most popular with people in Korea?
3. What does the name "Gwanseeum Bosal" translate as?
4. Why is Avalokitesvara sometimes depicted with a thousand hands and eyes?
5. What did Ksitigarbha Bodhisattva vow?
6. What do the ten kings do to the deceased according to Korean folk beliefs?
7. Does Ksitigarbha protect those who are lost in the underworld?

14 전각 3

무량수전(극락전)

아미타불을 모신 이 전각은 '무량수전' 또는 '극락전'이라고 불린다. '아미타바 (Amitabha)'는 산스크리트어로 '무량광(無量光)'을 의미하며, 또 다른 이름인 '아미타유스 (Amitayus)'는 '무량수(無量壽)'를 의미한다. 아미타불은 사람들이 죽은 후 이들을 자신의 서방정토로 이끌어준다. 악한 사람도 아미타불에게 간절히 기원하면 서방정토로 갈 수 있다. 정토란 불보살이 항상 거하며 고통이 없는 곳이다. 이곳에선 항상 꽃이 피고 새들도 법을 노래한다. 정토는 사람들이 부처가 될 수 있는 곳으로 다시 태어나기에는 가장 좋은 장소이다. 무량수전에서 아미타불의 협시보살은 대체로 관세음보살과 대세지보살이다.

약사전

약사전에 모신 약사여래는 질병을 치료한다. 약사여래는 또한 탐·진·치의 독도 치유해준다고 한다. 약사여래의 손에는 세상의 불행과 재난을 치유해줄 약병이 들려 있다. 사람들이 약사여래의 명호를 외고 진심으로 가호를 기원하면 재액을 막아주고 질병을 치유해준다고 믿기 때문에 약사여래는 일반인들이 매우 따르는 부처님이다. 약사여래의 왼쪽에는 월광보살이 오른쪽에는 일광보살이 모셔져 있다.

Unit 14 Temple Shrines III

Amitabha Hall (Muryangsu-jeon or Geungnak-jeon)

Dedicated to Amitabha Buddha, this hall is also called "Hall of Immeasurable Life" or "Hall of Western Paradise." Amitabha, in Sanskrit, means "immeasurable light," and his another name Amithayus means "immeasurable life." Amitabha Buddha is believed to lead beings to his Pure Land after death. Even a wicked person can go to the Pure Land if he petitions sincerely to Amitabha Buddha. The Pure Land is a place where buddhas and bodhisattvas are thought to reside, and where there is no suffering. Flowers bloom all the time, and even birds sing the Dharma. It is a place where one can become a buddha and is the best place to be reborn. In this hall, Amitabha is usually flanked by Avalokitesvara and Mahasthamaprapta (Daeseji Bosal).

Medicine Buddha Hall (Yaksa-jeon)

This hall is dedicated to the Medicine Buddha who cures disease and sickness. He is also believed to heal the inner poisons of greed, hatred, and ignorance. In his hand, he holds a jar of medicine to remedy the ills of the world. Medicine Buddha is very popular with people as they believe he can ward off all disasters and heal disease if they recite his name and petition for his protection.

Enshrined to the left of the Medicine Buddha is Candra-prabha, or Moonlight Bodhisattva (Wolgwang Bosal), and to the left is Surya-prabha, or Sunlight Bodhisattva (Ilgwang Bosal).

Fill in the Blanks

Dedicated to Amitabha Buddha, this hall is also called "Hall of _____ _____." (서방극락, 극락)

Amitabha, in Sanskrit, means "_____ _____." (무량광)

Amitabha Buddha is believed to lead beings to his _____ _____ after death. (정토)

Even a wicked person can go to the Pure Land if he _____ sincerely to Amitabha Buddha. (빌다, 청하다)

The Pure Land is a place where buddhas and bodhisattvas are thought to _____. (거주하다)

Flowers bloom all the time, and even birds _____ the Dharma. (노래하다)

It is the best place to be _____. (다시 태어나다)

This hall is dedicated to the Medicine Buddha who _____ disease and sickness. (치료하다)

He is also believed to _____ the inner poisons of greed, hatred, and ignorance. (치유하다)

In his hand, he holds a _____ of medicine to remedy the ills of the world.

(병)

192

People believe Medicine Buddha can _____ _____ all disasters and heal disease. (막아주다)

If they _____ _____ _____ and petition for his protection.

(명호를 외우다)

Medicine Buddha is flanked by Candra-prabha or _____ Bodhisattva and Surya-prabha or _____ Bodhisattva. (월광) (일광)

Questions
1. What does Amitabha mean?
2. Where does Amitabha lead the deceased to?
3. What qualities does the Pure Land of Amitabha have?
4. Which Buddha triad does the Amitabha Hall have?
5. Does the Medicine Buddha only heal physical diseases?
6. What does the Medicine Buddha hold in his hand?
7. Who is the Medicine Buddha flanked by?

전각 4

미륵전

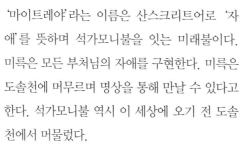

'마이트레야'라는 이름은 산스크리트어로 '자애'를 뜻하며 석가모니불을 잇는 미래불이다. 미륵은 모든 부처님의 자애를 구현한다. 미륵은 도솔천에 머무르며 명상을 통해 만날 수 있다고 한다. 석가모니불 역시 이 세상에 오기 전 도솔천에서 머물렀다.

미륵은 미래 어느 날 용화수 아래서 깨달음을 얻을 것이며 그런 후에는 법륜을 굴려 30억 중생을 커다란 사랑으로 구제할 것이라고한다.

나한전(응진각)

나한전은 탐·진·치의 삼독을 여읜 아라한을 모신 곳이다. 이곳에 모신 나한은 16분, 18분 또는 500분에 이르기도 한다. 나한은 보통 스님들의 모습으로 소박한 옷을 입고 있다. 나한은 초기불교와 현대 상좌부불교의 이상이다. 나한은 개인적인 깨달음의 증득을 강조한다.

Unit 15 Temple Shrines IV

Maitreya Buddha Hall (Mireuk-jeon)

"Maitreya" (Mireuk) means "loving-kindness," and is the "Future Buddha" who is a successor to Sakyamuni Buddha. Maitreya is the embodiment of all the buddhas' loving kindness. Maitreya resides in Tusita Heaven, and is said to be reachable through meditation. Sakyamuni Buddha also lived there before he was born into the world.

It is said that one day Maitreya will become enlightened under the dragon-flower tree (naga-puspa, Yonghwa-su) and turn the wheel of Dharma to save three billion souls with his great love.

Hall of Arhats (Nahan-jcon)

This is dedicated to arhats who have destroyed the three poisons of greed, hatred, and ignorance. The number of arhats represented in these halls can range from sixteen to eighteen to 500. Arhats are usually depicted in simple attire and in the form of monks. Arhats are the ideal of the early Buddhist era and modern Theravada Buddhism. Arhats emphasize the personal attainment of enlightenment.

Fill in the Blanks

"Maitreya" means "_____." (자애)

He is the "Future Buddha" who is a _____ to Buddha Sakyamuni. (계승자)

Maitreya is the _____ of all the buddhas' loving-kindness. (구현)

Maitreya resides in _____ _____. (도솔천)

Sakyamuni Buddha also lived there before he was born into the _____.

(세상)

It is said that one day Maitreya will become enlightened under the dragon-flower tree and turn the _____ of _____. (법륜)

This is dedicated to _____ who have destroyed the three poisons of greed, hatred, and ignorance. (아라한들)

Arhats are usually depicted in simple _____ and in the form of monks.

(복장)

Arhats are the ideal of the early Buddhist era and modern _____ Buddhism. (상좌부)

Arhats emphasize the _____ attainment of enlightenment. (개인적)

Questions

1. What does "Maitreya" mean?
2. Is Maitreya the Past Buddha?
3. Where does Maitreya reside?
4. Did Sakyamuni Buddha live in Tusita Heaven before he was born into the world?
5. Where will Maitreya become enlightened?
6. How many arhats are usually enshrined in the Hall of Arhats?
7. Which Buddhist tradition upholds arhats as an ideal?

Where does Maitreya reside?

16 전각 5

조사전

조사전은 절이나 법맥의 창건 또는 복원에 큰 공을 세운 고승들을 모신 곳이다. 조사란 법맥을 창건한 위대한 스님, 법맥을 전수받은 스님 또는 청정하고 고결한 스님을 말한다. 선종 사찰에서는 고승이 돌아가시면 부도를 세우고 영정을 조사전에 모신다. 국사를 배출한 절에는 조사전 대신 국사전을 세운다.

삼성각

삼성이란 칠성, 독성, 산신을 말한다. 이 삼성을 각기 독립된 사당에 모시기도 한다. 세 분 모두 한국 민간신앙의 주요 신격으로서 불교에 유입되었다. 칠성은 본래 도교에서 숭배하던 신으로서 아이들의 장수를 칠성님께 기원한다. 독성은 중국 천태산에서 깨달음을 얻은 나한이다. 한국불교에서 독성은 사람들을 돕는 신이다. 불화에서 독성은 흰 수염과 긴 눈썹을 가진 할아버지로 묘사된다. 산신은 산악지역이 많은 고대 한국에서 많은 영향력을 발휘한 신이다. 사찰들이 주로 산중에 있기 때문에 사찰에서는 지역 산신을 잘 모시기 위해 노력한다. 산신은 흔히 호랑이와 함께 있는 것으로 묘사된다.

Unit 16 Temple Shrines V

Hall of Patriarchs (Josa-jeon)

This hall is dedicated to eminent monks who played an important role in the establishment or revival of a temple or Buddhist order. A patriarch can be a great monk who established an order, a lineage holder (one who transmits the Dharma), or simply a moral and upstanding monk.

In Seon temples, when eminent monks pass away, a memorial stupa is established, and their portraits are enshrined in the Hall of Patriarchs. In temples where National Masters were produced, a Hall of National Masters (Guksa-jeon) is found instead of a Hall of Patriarchs.

Shrine of the Three Sages (Samseong-gak)

The three sages are the Big Dipper God (Chilseong), the Hermit Sage (Dokseong), and the Mountain God (Sansin). There will often be a hall dedicated to each figure. All three of these were prominent deities from the

Korean folk religion that were adopted by Buddhism.

The Big Dipper God originated in Daoism. People would pray to the Big Dipper God for their children to live long.

The Hermit Sage is an arhat, who is said to have attained enlightenment on Tiantai Mountain in China. In Korean Buddhism, he is considered to be a sage who benefits others. He is depicted in Buddhist paintings as an old man with a white beard and long eyebrows.

The Mountain God was an influential figure in ancient Korea because of the mountainous terrain. The Mountain God receives particular recognition in an attempt to appease the local mountain spirits, on whose land the temple stands. The Mountain God is commonly depicted with a tiger.

Fill in the **B**lanks

This hall is dedicated to _____ _____ . (고승들)

They played an important role in the _____ or _____ of a temple or Buddhist order. (창건) (복원)

A _____ can be a great monk who established an order or a lineage holder. (조사)

In Seon temples, when eminent monks pass away, a _____ _____ is established. (부도)

Their _____ are enshrined in the Hall of Patriarchs. (영정, 초상)

In temples where _____ _____ were produced, a Hall of National Masters (Guksa-jeon) is found. (국사)

The _____ _____ are the Big Dipper God (Chilseong), the Hermit Sage (Dokseong), and the Mountain God (Sansin). (삼성)

All three of these were prominent deities from the Korean _____ _____ that were adopted by Buddhism. (민간신앙)

The Big Dipper God originated in _____. (도교)

People would pray to the Big Dipper God for their children to _____

_____. (장수하다)

The Hermit Sage is depicted in _____ _____ as an old man with a

_____ _____ and long eyebrows. (불화) (흰 수염)

The Mountain God was an _____ figure in ancient Korea because of the

mountainous terrain. (영향력 있는)

The Mountain God is commonly depicted with a _____. (호랑이)

Questions

1. What is a patriarch?
2. Is the Hall of Patriarchs dedicated to very eminent monks?
3. Can you find a portrait of a National Master in the Hall of Patriarchs?
4. Did the three sages originate in Buddhism?
5. Which sage attained enlightenment on Tiantai Mountain?
6. Which sage is usually depicted with a tiger?
7. Which sage do you pray to if you want a long life for your child?

불교영어 초급1

1판 1쇄 펴냄 | 2012년 3월 5일
개정판 1쇄 펴냄 | 2015년 1월 30일
개정판 3쇄 펴냄 | 2020년 4월 10일

편찬 | 대한불교조계종 교육원 불학연구소
집필 | 대한불교조계종 교육원 불학연구소(1부) · 한국불교영어번역연구원(2부, 3부)
번역 | 한국불교영어번역연구원
총괄감수 | 진우기

발행인 | 정지현
편집인 | 박주혜
사장 | 최승천

펴낸곳 | (주)조계종출판사
출판등록 | 제2007-000078호(2007.4.27)
주소 | 서울시 종로구 삼봉로 81 두산위브파빌리온 232호
전화 | 02-720-6107~9
팩스 | 02-733-6708
구입문의 | 불교전문서점(www.jbbook.co.kr) 02-2031-2070~1

ISBN 978-89-93629-80-4 (세트)
   979-11-5580-032- 4 04740